"My husband and I are either going to buy a dog or have a child. We can't decide whether to ruin our carpets or ruin our lives."   —Rita Rudner

At once laugh-out-loud and irresistibly heartwarming, Speak! *offers wit and wisdom from famous and not-so-famous dog lovers through the ages. From Abraham Lincoln to Oprah Winfrey, Mark Twain to Lyndon Johnson, Ulysses S. Grant to Jimmy Stewart, these clever quips and touching tales offer a unique tribute to the four-legged friends who have stolen our hearts . . .*

"For me a house or an apartment becomes a home when you add one set of four legs, a happy tail, and that indescribable measure of love that we call a dog."   —Roger Caras

"I can train any dog in five minutes. It's training the owner that takes longer."   —Barbara Woodhouse

"Dogs act exactly the way we would act if we had no shame."
—Cynthia Heimel

"If you don't want your dog to have bad breath, do what I do: Pour a little Lavoris in the toilet."   —Jay Leno

"You want a friend in this town? Get a dog!" —Harry S. Truman

CONNIE DUBAY is a longtime dog lover whose best childhood friend was a Pomeranian. When n̶̶ uate school and is a business con̶̶ with her husband and her retrieve̶̶

D1057326

Speak!

The Best Quips, Quotes, and Anecdotes for Dog Lovers

Compiled and Edited by
Connie DuBay

A PLUME BOOK

PLUME
Published by the Penguin Group
Penguin Putnam Inc., 375 Hudson Street,
New York, New York 10014, U.S.A.
Penguin Books Ltd, 27 Wrights Lane, London W8 5TZ, England
Penguin Books Australia Ltd, Ringwood, Victoria, Australia
Penguin Books Canada Ltd, 10 Alcorn Avenue,
Toronto, Ontario, Canada M4V 3B2
Penguin Books (N.Z.) Ltd, 182–190 Wairau Road,
Auckland 10, New Zealand

Penguin Books Ltd, Registered Offices:
Harmondsworth, Middlesex, England

First published by Plume, a member of Penguin Putnam Inc.

First Printing, November 2000
1   3   5   7   9   10   8   6   4   2

LIBRARY OF CONGRESS CATALOGING-IN-PUBLICATION DATA:

Speak! : the best quips, quotes, and anecdotes for dog lovers /
[compiled by] Connie DuBay.
    p.   cm.
  ISBN 0-452-28205-5
  1. Dogs—Quotations, maxims, etc. I. DuBay, Connie.
PN6084.D64 S69 2000
636.7—dc21   00-031373

Printed in the United States of America
Set in Souvenir Light

*For my husband, Jim Peterson, who loves dogs
as much as I do, and for Reily, who
doesn't think he is one.*

Generally, or at least very often, people with a deep interest in animals are the best people around.

—Roger Caras, author, president emeritus of ASPCA (b. 1928)

CONTENTS

ACKNOWLEDGMENTS

I am grateful to the many people who helped make *Speak!* a reality. Thanks to:

Sheree Bykofsky, for her valuable insights, not only as my agent but also as a fellow dog lover, and Janet Rosen who worked with me at the early stages of this project. Elaine Partnow for her kinds words of advice.

All the folks at Plume publishing, with special thanks to Jennifer Dickerson Kasius, Rosemary Ahern, and Sara Bixler for their constructive feedback and ability to keep all the details together that go into the publication of a book.

All the trainers, breeders, veterinarians and other

dog lovers who are committed to the humane treatment of animals as fellow creatures on this planet. Especially to Marge Gibbs, who taught me a trick or two about training Reily.

My family and friends for their greatly appreciated encouragement. Space limitations prevent me from listing everyone but my love and thanks to you all. Most notably, my mother, Millie DuBay, who gave me a love for literature; my father, Bernard DuBay, who gave me a love for animals; my sister, Candace DuBay, who cheered me on; and Joyce Watts, my mentor and friend over many, many years, who inspired me to start writing again after a long hiatus.

Lastly, never-ending thanks go to Jim Peterson, my husband and biggest fan, for his loving support and immensely helpful input over the course of this project.

AUTHOR'S NOTE

I have inserted biographical information below each quote to show that the special connection between humans and dogs has spanned centuries and continents. Whenever national origin does not appear in the biographical information it is because the individual quoted is (or was) from the United States. This reference was deleted in order to avoid redundancy, since a large number of individuals quoted share the U.S. as their national origin. I hope that you enjoy reading this collection of quotes as much as I enjoyed collecting them.

INTRODUCTION

We love dogs. Is it any wonder that we do? Dogs have been our loyal companions throughout history; they have stood by the sides of the famous and not so famous, the rich and the poor, the brilliant and the ordinary humans they have befriended.

As ever-faithful friends over the centuries, dogs have witnessed human history from an uncommon perspective. There was Charlie, Kennedy's Welsh terrier, in the oval office during the Cuban Missile crisis; Fala, Roosevelt's Scottie, on a World War II warship in the middle of the Atlantic during the signing of the Atlantic Charter; Diamond, Sir Isaac Newton's

Pomeranian who was present when the law of gravity was discovered; and an unknown Newfoundland who actually saved Napoleon's life!

Courageous, loyal, nonjudgmental, forgiving, joyful and living ever in the present a dog's relationship with us carries no pretense, no baggage from the past, and no hidden agendas. With our dogs we are free to be ourselves and they love us for who we are, not what we are.

So it shouldn't be surprising that dogs continue to be so popular. In the United States alone there are over 40 million dogs, which is an average of one dog for every two households. Dog loving England and France follow.

One only needs to look at the English language to realize how much dogs are and have almost always been a part of our lives. We work like a dog, have a dog's chance, recognize that the workplace is dog eat dog, and if we get promoted, we become a lucky dog. At a restaurant, many of us put on the dog, and after dining, we take home doggie bags. When playing golf the fairways may have a dogleg to the right or left. If we have an argument with a spouse, we're in the dog-house.

Although dogs have been man's and woman's best friend for centuries, our relationship with them has changed over time from hunting and working dogs in the fields to companion dogs in our homes. Not only have they moved inside the house but they have become members of the family in our hearts. Evidence of this is the large percentage of dog owners who carry a picture of their dog in their wallet and an estimated one million Americans who have named their dogs in their wills.

We also put our wallets where our hearts are by spending $21 billion each year on the care of our pets. The demand for everything dog related is evidenced by the plethora of products and services that have made noticeable appearances in the last few years. Doggie day-care, puppy memory books, pet sitters, chain pet stores, dog web sites, gourmet dog treats, down filled beds, dog photographers, dog clothing, dog Halloween costumes, dog perfume, dog shrinks, poochie Prozac and deluxe dog-friendly hotels. And of course let's not forget about *Millie's Book*. Where else could a book by the first family's springer spaniel outsell the memoirs of the dog's owner, former President George Bush?

As members of the family, dogs share our lives in ways they never have before. They are shaping our culture and the way we live. Thanks to dog-friendly employers, we can now bring our dogs to work with us. We jog, rollerblade and bicycle with our dogs. We teach our dogs stupid pet tricks. When evening comes, many of us feel secure having our dogs sleep by our side.

Reading this book validates our feelings and shows us that we are not alone in having an emotional connection with our four-legged companions. Not only are we not alone, but we are also not as crazy as some of our friends and relatives without dogs would have us believe! After all, if Freud, Churchill, Picasso and a host of others loved their dogs, then it must be okay for us to love ours too.

Speak! The Best Quips, Quotes, and Anecdotes for Dog Lovers looks at our relationship with dogs over the centuries. It is a collection of thoughts from the famous and not so famous who, despite all their differences, share one thing in common—all have experienced a strong emotional bond with a dog.

I first began collecting quotes about dogs for an article that I planned to write. However, through my research I quickly became fascinated by the number of people over the centuries who clearly loved dogs and had something interesting to say about our canine companions. These individuals include business people, theologians, philosophers, saints, writers, actors, actresses, comedians, inventors, scientists, athletes, presidents, heads of state, military leaders and entertainers. Among them are Pulitzer, Nobel Prize, Oscar, Emmy, Grammy, as well as other significant award winners in their chosen field. What started out as a trip to the library to collect a few quotes became a labor of love, pouring over hundreds of books, articles and other reference materials. The result of all this is *Speak!*

The quips, quotes, and anecdotes in this book reveal that for dogs who are fortunate enough to be with people who truly love them, a dog's life is a pretty wonderful life. Organized in a way that will be meaningful to any dog owner, *Speak!* covers all aspects of the life we share with our furry friends. The book begins with our first thoughts of getting a pet. It then covers both the joyful major events and routine daily activities that come with dog ownership. The final chapter, "Saying Good-bye," tackles the tough spiritual question "Do dogs go to heaven?" *Speak!* celebrates the special place that dogs have in our hearts.

1
Getting a Dog

Selecting and Naming Your Pet

My husband and I are either going to buy a dog or have a child. We can't decide whether to ruin our carpets or ruin our lives. —*Rita Rudner, comedian (b. 1955)*

Happiness is a warm puppy.
—*Charles M. Schultz, cartoonist (1922–2000)*

Whoever said you can't buy happiness forgot about puppies. —*Gene Hill, columnist and author (1928–1997)*

[Being a parent] is tough. If you just want a wonderful little creature to love, you can get a puppy.

—*Barbara Walters, broadcast journalist (b. 1931)*

Buy a pup and your money will buy love unflinching.

—*Rudyard Kipling, Indian-born British author (1865–1936)*

What's the difference between a 3-week-old puppy and a sportswriter? In 6 weeks, the puppy will stop whining. —*Mike Ditka, football player and coach (b. 1939)*

The biggest dog has been a pup.

—*Joaquin Miller, poet (1839–1913)*

A puppy is but a dog, plus high spirits, and minus common sense. —*Agnes Repplier, essayist (1855–1950)*

The best way to get a puppy is to beg for a baby brother—and they'll settle for a puppy every time.

—*Winston Pendleton, author (b. 1910)*

Acquiring a dog may be the only opportunity a human ever has to choose a relative.

—*Mordecai Siegal, author (b. 1934)*

> **If you can't decide between a Shepherd, a Setter, or a Poodle, get them all. . . . Adopt a mutt.**
>
> —*American Society for the Prevention of Cruelty to Animals (ASPCA)*

You paused outside to look into my cage. I tried to play it right wanting to catch your eye with a shy glint in my own, a soft bark, that said, "Choose me," in a canine grammar I hoped you'd understand.

[Author's account of his dog Scout's adoption from a shelter] —R. S. Jones, writer (b. 1934)

I love to rescue animals. . . . The pounds were so crowded they were putting animals down almost immediately. Seven thousand dogs were put to sleep.

[Discussing how the big 1994 Northridge earthquake in L.A. impacted dogs and how she managed to save one of them] —Laura Dern, actress (b. 1967)

"Hi," I said. She came over, licked my hand discreetly, allowed herself to be scratched for a time, chased her tail in a dignified circle, lay down again. I remember thinking: "There are times God puts a choice in front of you." I often had such thoughts back then. We took the dog. —Stanley Bing, columnist for Fortune

Money will buy you a pretty good dog but it won't buy you the wag of his tail.

—*Henry Wheeler Shaw, humorist (1818–1885)*

From behind a wooden crate we saw a long black-muzzled nose poking round at us. We took him out—soft, wobbly, tearful; set him down on his four, as yet not quite simultaneous legs, and regarded him. He wandered a little round our legs, neither wagging his tail nor licking at our hands; then he looked up, and my companion said: "He's an angel!"

—*John Galsworthy, English novelist and playwright (1867–1933)*

Thank God I got the rejects. These animals are very, very affectionate.

[Speaking about how she got her two poodles from a breeder who thought that the puppies weren't up to standard]

—*Eartha Kitt, actress and singer (b. 1927)*

I very much believe in rescuing animals, not buying them.

[She found her dog, Lois, a terrier and basset hound mix] —*Candice Bergen, actress (b. 1946)*

I need a dog pretty badly. I dreamed of dogs last night. They sat in a circle and looked at me and I wanted all of them. —*John Steinbeck, novelist (1902–1968)*

My name is Oprah Winfrey. I have a talk show. I'm single. I have eight dogs—five golden retrievers, two black labs, and a mongrel. I have four years of college.

[Oprah Winfrey's answer when asked to describe herself in a Chicago federal courtroom during the jury selection process. She appeared when requested for possible jury duty.]

—*Oprah Winfrey, talk-show host (b. 1953)*

I've been on so many blind dates, I should get a free dog. —*Wendy Liebman, comedian*

Any man with money to make the purchase can become a dog's owner. But no man—spend he ever so much coin and food and tact in the effort—may become a dog's Master without the consent of the dog. Do you get the difference? And he whom a dog once unreservedly accepts as Master is forever that dog's God.

—*Albert Payson Terhune, author (1872–1942)*

Every puppy should have a boy.

—*Erma Bombeck, author and humorist (1927–1996)*

Give a boy a dog and you've furnished him a play-mate.
—*Berton Braley, author (1882–1966)*

The ideal age for a boy to own a dog is between forty-five and fifty.
—*Robert Benchley, actor and author (1889–1945)*

A house is not a home until it has a dog.
—*Gerald Durrell, British zoologist (1925–1995)*

Our house was always filled with dogs. . . . They helped make our house a kennel, it is true, but the constant patter of their filthy paws and the dreadful results of their brainless activities have warmed me throughout the years.
—*Helen Hayes, actress (1900–1993)*

It is home to a dog after he has been there three nights.
—*Finnish proverb*

NAME

ADDRESS

CITY

STATE ____ ZIP ____

☐ CHECK HERE IF NEW ADDRESS

BUSINESS REPLY MAIL

FIRST CLASS PERMIT NO. 03708   CHELMSFORD, MA

POSTAGE WILL BE PAID BY ADDRESSEE

IN THE COMPANY OF

DOGS

CUSTOMER SERVICE
222 MILL ROAD
CHELMSFORD, MA 01824-3692

IMPORTANT: If you wish to have your order filled within the next 30 days or sooner, please do not return this card.

DATE   MAY 5, 2003

ORDER #   P3713526000000   NAME   MICHELLE L BROWN

STYLE #   DESCRIPTION

D50088   FOXY LADY BAG

PLEASE CANCEL ONLY THE ITEM(S)
I HAVE CHECKED BELOW

DUE 05/09/03

A man down in Texas heard Pat on the radio mention the fact that our two daughters would like to have a dog. And believe it or not, the day before we left on this campaign trip we got a message from Union Station in Baltimore saying they had a package for us. We went down to get it. You know what it was? It was a little cocker spaniel in a crate that he sent all the way from Texas. . . . And our little girl Tricia, the six-year-old, named it Checkers. And you know the kids love the dog and I just want to say this, right now, that regardless of what they [the Press] have to say about it, we are going to keep it.

[Nixon spoke on television about the cocker spaniel that was given to him after he was accused of accepting improper gifts in what later became known as the Checkers speech, September 23, 1952. The speech saved Nixon's political career and made Checkers one of the most famous dogs in political history. Three years after Nixon died, the body of Checkers (who died in 1964) was ex-humed from its resting place on Long Island and moved to the grounds of the Nixon Library and re-

buried near the graves of the late president and his wife.]   —*Richard M. Nixon, 37th president (1913–1994)*

A person who has never owned a dog has missed a wonderful part of life.

> —*Bob Barker, television personality and animal-rights activist (b. 1923)*

I am joy in a wooly coat, come to dance into your life, to make you laugh!   —*Julie Church, author*

To be followed home by a stray dog is a sign of impending wealth.   —*Chinese proverb*

We never really own a dog as much as he owns us.

> —*Gene Hill, columnist and author (1928–1997)*

You become responsible forever, for what you have tamed.

—*Antoine de Saint-Exupéry, French author*
and aviator (1900–1944)

A dog is for life, and not just for Christmas.

—*Slogan of the National Canine Defense League*

The country at large takes a natural interest in the President's dogs and judges him by the taste and discrimination he shows in his selection . . . any man who does not like dogs and want them about does not deserve to be in the White House.

—American Kennel Club Gazette, 1924

For me a house or an apartment becomes a home when you add one set of four legs, a happy tail, and that indescribable measure of love that we call a dog.

—*Roger Caras, author and president*
emeritus of the ASPCA (b. 1928)

Aristocrats have heirs, the poor have children, and the rest keep dogs.

—*Spike Milligan, Irish comedian and author (b. 1918)*

No man can be condemned for owning a dog. As long as he has a dog, he has a friend; and the poorer he gets, the better friend he has.

—*Will Rogers, actor and humorist (1879–1935)*

Not Carnegie, Vanderbilt and Astor together could have raised money enough to buy a quarter share in my little dog.

—*Ernest Thompson Seton, naturalist and writer (1860–1946)*

> **No matter how little money and how few possessions you own, having a dog makes you rich.**
>
> —*Louis Sabin, author (b. 1930)*

Like many other much-loved humans, they believed that they owned their dogs, instead of realizing that their dogs owned them.

[From 101 Dalmatians*]*

—*Dodie Smith, English writer (1896–1990)*

Dogs are a habit, I think.

—*Elizabeth Bowen, author (1899–1973)*

Why own a dog? There's a danger you know,
You can't own just one, for the craving will grow.

There's no doubt they're addictive, wherein lies the danger.
While living with lots, you'll grow poorer and stranger.

—*Author unknown*

You should keep dogs—fine animals—sagacious.

—*Charles Dickens, English author (1812–1870)*

If you don't own a dog, at least one, there is not necessarily anything wrong with you, but there may be something wrong with your life.

—*Roger Caras, author and president emeritus of the ASPCA (b. 1928)*

Great men always have dogs.

—*Ouida, English author (1839–1908)*

I am his Highness' dog at Kew;
Pray tell me sir, whose dog are you?
  [Engraved on the collar of a dog given to the Prince of Wales (his residence was at Kew)]
    —*Alexander Pope, English poet and satirist (1688–1744)*

Pray steal me not, I'm Mrs. Dingley's,
Whose heart in this four-footed thing lies.
  [Inscription on the collar of a lapdog]
    —*Jonathan Swift, Irish author and satirist (1667–1745)*

My advice to any diplomat who wants to have good press is to have two or three kids and a dog.
    —*Carl Rowan, journalist (b. 1925)*

I stand fearlessly for small dogs, the American flag, motherhood and the Bible. That's why people love me.

—*Art Linkletter, television personality (b. 1912)*

During the Prince's visit, King Timahoe will be referred to only as Timahoe, since it would be inappropriate for the Prince to be outranked by a dog.

[A note to the White House staff on how to handle the name of the president's Irish setter, King Timahoe, during a visit by Prince Charles of Britain]

—*Richard M. Nixon, 37th president of the United States (1913–1994)*

His name is Rufus II—but the II is silent.

[Churchill talking about the name of his second

poodle. *After the death of his first poodle, Churchill got another and, like the first, named it Rufus.*]

—Winston Churchill, *British statesman and prime minister (1874–1965)*

I spilled spot remover on my dog. He's gone now. —*Steven Wright, Canadian comedian (b. 1955)*

2
Dog Days

The Routine: Play, Walks, Sex,
Sleep, Food, Dogfights

Play

The great pleasure of a dog is that you may make a fool of yourself with him and not only will he not scold you, but he will make a fool out of himself too.

—*Samuel Butler, English author and satirist (1835–1902)*

I think we are drawn to dogs because they are the uninhibited creatures we might be if we weren't certain we knew better.   —*George Bird Evans, author (b. 1906)*

Man is troubled by what might be called the Dog Wish, a strange and involved compulsion to be as happy and carefree as a dog.

—*James Thurber, author and cartoonist (1894–1961)*

In order to really enjoy a dog, one doesn't merely train him to be semi-human. The point of it is to open oneself to the possibility of becoming part dog.

—*Edward Hoagland, naturalist and author (b. 1932)*

When a doting person gets down on all fours and plays with the dog's rubber mouse, it only confuses the puppy and gives him a sense of insecurity. He gets the impression that the world is unstable and wonders whether he is supposed to walk on his hind legs and smoke cigars.

—*Corey Ford, humorist and author (1902–1969)*

Dogs laugh, but they laugh with their tails . . . what puts man in a higher state of evolution is that he has got his laugh on the right end.

—*Max Eastman, editor and writer (1883–1969)*

It is fatal to let any dog know that he is funny, for he immediately loses his head and starts hamming it up.

—*Sir Pelham Grenville Wodehouse, English-born American humorist and author (1881–1975)*

'Twould make a dog laugh.

—*John Payne Collier, English editor (1789–1883)*

A dog wags its tail with its heart.

—*Martin Buxbaum, writer (1919–1991)*

Did you ever walk into a room and forget why you walked in? I think that's how dogs spend their lives.

—*Sue Murphy, comedian*

A door is what a dog is perpetually on the wrong side of.
—*Ogden Nash, poet (1902–1971)*

The dog has got more fun out of man than man has got out of the dog, for the clearly demonstrable reason that man is the more laughable of the two animals.
—*James Thurber, author and cartoonist (1894–1961)*

If you are a dog and your owner suggests that you wear a sweater . . . suggest that he wear a tail.
—*Fran Lebowitz, journalist (b. 1951)*

I dressed *dear sweet little Dash* for the second time after dinner in a scarlet jacket and blue trousers.
[On her King Charles cavalier spaniel, Dash]
—*Queen Victoria, British royalty (1819–1901)*

In regard to dogs, my most memorable thoughts concern my daughter's dog and her fondness for them. In fact, one day while working at the office, she hosted a birthday party for one of her Newfoundlands and the party was attended by dogs of other coworkers. It was a hectic few hours, but I believe the guests enjoyed themselves.

—*Thomas. S. Monaghan, founder and former chairman of Domino's Pizza (b. 1937)*

Scratch a dog and you'll find a permanent job. —*Franklin P. Jones, businessman (1887–1929)*

I know at last what distinguishes man from animals: financial worries.

—*Romain Rolland, French author and biographer (1866–1944)*

Dogs lead a nice life. You never see a dog with a wristwatch. —*George Carlin, comedian (b. 1937)*

In a dog-eat-dog world, it is the dogmatic domain of dog lovers to offer dogdom a dog's chance to rise above the dog days for a doggone good time.

—American Kennel Club Gazette

Dogs act exactly the way we would act if we had no shame. —*Cynthia Heimel, writer and humorist (b. 1947)*

If you play with the dog, he will lick your face.

—*Vietnamese proverb*

It was a fine fall morning in Paris, crisp and clear, and Benji was quite full of himself, cavorting near the fountain, playing with the children who had inexplicably materialized out of nowhere at the first whiff of a movie star. Their faces radiated and they took turns gently stroking his head. Those Benji chose to favor with a big sloppy lick exploded with laughter, and one young girl ran to her mother, screeching in French that she would never wash her face again.

—*Joe Camp, writer and producer/director of* Benji *(b.1939)*

I have caught more ills from people sneezing over me and giving me virus infections than from kissing dogs.

—*Barbara Woodhouse, Irish professional dog trainer (1910–1988)*

The dog was created specifically for children. He is the god of frolic.

—*Henry Ward Beecher, clergyman (1813–1887)*

Happiness is dog-shaped, I say.

—*Chapman Pincher, Indian author (b. 1914)*

No symphony orchestra ever played music like a two-year-old girl laughing with a puppy.

—*Bern Williams, English philosopher and Oxford University professor (b. 1929)*

He had let out the dogs and they were jumping around him frantic with joy, as if they were afraid, every night, there would never be another letting out or another morning. —*Mary O'Hara, writer (1885–1980)*

The most affectionate creature in the world is a wet dog.

—*Ambrose Bierce, journalist, editor, and author (1842–1914)*

Anybody who doesn't know what soap tastes like never washed a dog.

—*Franklin P. Jones, businessman (1887–1929)*

Dogs who chase cars evidently see them as large, unruly ungulates badly in need of discipline and shepherding.   —*Elizabeth Marshall Thomas, writer (b. 1931)*

[Being a celebrity] doesn't even seem to keep the fleas off our dogs—and if being a celebrity won't give me an advantage over a couple of fleas, then I guess there can't be much in being a celebrity after all.

—*Walt Disney, movie producer (1901–1966)*

Let Hercules himself do what he may,
The cat will mew and dog will have his day.

—*William Shakespeare, English dramatist and poet (1564–1616)*

Every dog has his day.   —*English proverb*

> **About the only thing on a farm that has an easy time is the dog.**
>
> —*Edgar Watson Howe, journalist (1853–1937)*

Walks

Elizabeth's back at the Red Cross, and I'm walking the dog.

[Describing life after the 1996 elections on the Today *show]*

> —*Bob Dole, former U.S. senator and presidential candidate (b. 1923)*

I took my dog for a walk . . . all the way from New York to Florida. . . . I said to him "There, now you're done."   —*Steven Wright, Canadian comedian (b. 1955)*

Golf seems to be an arduous way to go for a walk. I prefer to take the dogs out.

—*Princess Anne, British royalty (b. 1950)*

You know why dogs have no money? No pockets. 'Cause they see change on the street all the time and it's driving them crazy. When you're walking them, he is always looking up at you. "There's a quarter. . . ."

—*Jerry Seinfeld, comedian (b. 1954)*

Some of our greatest historical and artistic treasures we place with curators in museums; others we take for walks.

—*Roger Caras, author and president emeritus of the ASPCA (b. 1928)*

If your dog is fat, you aren't getting enough exercise.
                                            —*Author unknown*

A dog is one of the remaining reasons why some people can be persuaded to go for a walk.
                    —*O. A. Battista, Canadian author (b. 1917)*

When he came up two days short, he didn't get a dog. That was harsh. It was wise, but harsh.
    [Chris Affleck, talking about how she responded when her son Ben wanted a dog as a boy. She had him walk an imaginary mutt for a week.]
                    —*Chris Affleck, mother of actor Ben Affleck*

Every time I told my Cocker Spaniel, Taffy, my very first dog, that we were going for a walk, she would launch into a celebratory dance that ended with her racing around the room, always clockwise, and faster and faster, as if her joy could not be possibly contained. Even as a young boy I knew that hardly any creature could express joy so vividly as a dog.

—*Jeffrey Moussaieff Masson, author (b. 1941)*

To a dog the whole world is a smell.

—*Author unknown*

A dog's nose is something for us to wonder at. It is perfectly remarkable and reminds us that there is a world out there that we can never know. At least not as human beings.

—*Roger Caras, author and president emeritus of the ASPCA (b. 1928)*

It is my experience that in some areas [my poodle] Charley is more intelligent than I am, but in others he is abysmally ignorant. He can't read, can't drive a car, and has no grasp of mathematics. But in his own field of endeavor, which he is now practicing, the slow, imperial smelling over and anointing of an area, he has no peer. Of course his horizons are limited, but how wide are mine?

—*John Steinbeck, novelist (1902–1968)*

Dogs need to sniff the ground; it's how they keep abreast of current events. The ground is a giant dog newspaper, containing all kinds of late-breaking dog news items, which, if they are especially urgent, are often continued in the next yard.

—*Dave Barry, humorist and columnist (b. 1947)*

Dog owners are out in all kinds of weather. They tell you it's small payment for the love their dogs bear them. Some love. If that dog weren't on a leash, he'd be off after another dog, a cat, or any stranger walking along the street with a wet bag of meat.

—*Selma Diamond, Canadian author (1920–1985)*

The other day I saw two dogs walk over to a parking meter. One of them says to the other, "How do you like that. Pay toilets!" —*Dave Starr, comedian*

Never stand between a dog and the hydrant.
—*John Peers, author*

The trees in Siberia are miles apart, that is why the dogs are so fast. —*Bob Hope, comedian and actor (b. 1903)*

I just bought a Chihuahua. It's the dog for lazy people. You don't have to walk it. Just hold it out the window and squeeze.

—*Anthony Clark, actor and comedian (b. 1964)*

The other day a dog peed on me. A bad sign.
—*H. L. Mencken, essayist and satirist (1880–1956)*

Arnold was a dog's dog. Whenever he shuffled along walks and through alleyways, he always gave the impression of being on to something big.

—*Martha Grimes, author (b. 1930)*

Oh, that dog! All he does is piddle. He's nothing but a fur-covered kidney that barks.

—*Phyllis Diller, comedian (b. 1917)*

Dogs are animals that poop in public and you're supposed to pick it up. After a week of doing this, you've got to ask yourself: "Who's the real master in this relationship?"

—*Anthony Griffin, comedian*

Sex

I say with all my heart that unless the owner of such a dog particularly requires it for show purposes, it should be neutered to make its life happy and that of its owners equally trouble free.

—Barbara Woodhouse, Irish professional dog trainer (1910–1988)

It's like this, dear boy, the one in front is blind and the kind one behind is pushing him.

[Explanation given to Laurence Olivier's young son when he saw two dogs copulating and asked what they were doing]

—Noël Coward, English playwright and actor (1899–1973)

I am cursed with a right leg that arouses the desire of any male dog that happens to be passing. I used to think that this only happened to me but I've discovered that many people have the same problem. They have a *femme fatale* limb.

—Jasper Carrott, British author (b. 1945)

Our late lamented English setter was spoilt, goofy, terrifyingly tenacious and possessed a totally unbridled sex drive. If he got on the trail of a bitch, he would charge across three main roads, race twenty miles until he caught up with her and then mount her from the wrong end. —*Jilly Cooper, English author (b. 1937)*

They say the dog is man's best friend. I don't believe that. How many of your friends have you neutered?
—*Larry Reeb, comedian*

I tried to get my dog to practice safe sex. But he keeps licking the condoms off. —*Tim Halpern, comedian*

Had he been Shakespeare, he would then have written *Troilus and Cressida* to brand the offending sex; but being only a little dog, he began to bite them.

[On his Skye terrier Woggs's reaction to being refused by female dogs]
—*Robert Louis Stevenson, Scottish author (1850–1894)*

She lies about her age and weight and is slightly older than Rocket. But they've been a couple for eight years, longer than most in Hollywood.

[On her two dogs, Catcher and Rocket]

—Kate Jackson, actress (b. 1948)

Sleep

You know there is no one in the world I would rather sleep with than Yuki.

[On his terrier, Yuki]

—Lyndon Baines Johnson, 36th president of the United States (1908–1973)

Let sleeping dogs lie. —*English proverb*

It is nought good a sleeping hound to wake.

—*Geoffrey Chaucer, English poet (c. 1343–1400)*

Whoever said "let sleeping dogs lie" didn't sleep with dogs. *—Author unknown*

Watson: Is there any point to which you would wish to draw my attention?

Holmes: To the curious incident of the dog in the nighttime.

Watson: The dog did nothing in the nighttime.

Holmes: That was the curious incident.

> *—Sir Arthur Conan Doyle, British author and physician (1859–1930)*

When a puppy takes fifty catnaps in the course of the day, he cannot always be expected to sleep the night through.

—Albert Payson Terhune, author (1872–1942)

The truth is that it's just really hard for me to get to sleep without a dog in my bedroom. . . . I once had a dog named Beau. He used to sleep in the corner of the bedroom. Some nights, though, he would sneak onto the bed and lie right between Gloria and me. I know that I should have pushed him off the bed, but I didn't. He was up there because he wanted me to pat his head, so that's what I would do.

—*Jimmy Stewart, actor (1908–1997)*

Did you hear about the dyslexic agnostic insomniac who stays awake all night wondering if there is a Dog?

—*Author unknown*

Like a dog, he hunts in his dreams.

—*Alfred Lord Tennyson, English poet (1809–1902)*

Even his sleep was full of dreams. He dreamt as he had not dreamt since the old days at Three Mile Cross—of hares starting from the long grass; of pheasants rocketing up with long tails streaming, of partridge rising with a whirr from the stubble. He dreamt that he was hunting, that he was chasing some spotted spaniel, who fled, who escaped him. . . . Then he opened his eyes. There were no hares, and no partridges; no whips cracking. . . . There was only Mr. Browning in the armchair talking to Miss Barrett on the sofa.

[Writing about the dreams of the dog, Flush, who was owned by Robert Browning and Elizabeth Barrett Browning. Woolf wrote a biography about the dog. Before Elizabeth met her husband, her dog Flush, a cocker spaniel, was dognapped and held for ransom, an unfortunate practice in Victorian England. Elizabeth, not having sufficient funds to pay, risked her own safety by going into a dangerous part of the city to negotiate directly with the dognappers. Flush was returned safely.]

—*Virginia Woolf, English author (1882–1941)*

If you lie down with dogs, you will get up with fleas.

—*Author unknown*

A dog teaches a boy fidelity, perseverance, and to turn around three times before lying down. —*Robert Benchley, actor and author (1889–1945)*

I can't imagine living in a house without a couple of dogs. If I ever got out of bed at night and didn't have to step over a Labrador or two or three, or move one off the covers so I could turn over, my nights would be more restless and the demons that wait in the dark for me would be less easily fended.

—*Gene Hill, columnist and author (1928–1997)*

And sometimes when you'd get up in the middle of the night you'd hear the reassuring thump, thump of her tail on the floor, letting you know that she was there and thinking of you.

—*William Cole, author (b. 1919)*

Food

If you think dogs can't count, try putting three dog biscuits in your pocket and then giving Fido only two of them. —*Phil Pastoret, comedian*

Woody: "How's it going, Mr. Peterson?"
Norm: "It's a dog eat dog world, Woody, and I'm wearing Milk Bone underwear."

—*From the TV show* Cheers

It freshens your breath and helps prevent tartar.
[After eating a dog biscuit in front of an audience at Harvard after being named "Man of the Year" by Hasty Pudding]
—*Mel Gibson, American-born Australian actor (b. 1956)*

Ever consider what they must think of us? I mean, here we come back from a grocery store with the most amazing haul—chicken, pork, half a cow. They must think we're the greatest hunters on earth!

—*Anne Tyler, author (b. 1941)*

A dog in the kitchen asks for no company.

—*French proverb*

Mrs. Bush had a rule about not giving Millie food at the table—which the President would often break. Millie would look at him with those eyes, and he couldn't resist.

—*Jean Becker, former President George Bush's chief of staff*

Ah, if I could only pray the way that dog looks at meat.

[On his dog Toelpel]

—*Martin Luther, German theologian (1438–1546)*

A well-trained dog will make no attempt to share your lunch. He will just make you feel so guilty that you cannot enjoy it.
—*Helen Thomson, English writer*

The dogs eat of the crumbs which fall from their master's table.
—*Matthew 5:27*

A dog will never forget the crumb thou gavest him.
—*Sa'di, Iranian poet (d. 1292)*

My dog is worried about the economy because Alpo is up to 99¢ a can. That's almost $7.00 in dog money.
—*Joe Weinstein, comedian*

There is no snooze button on a dog who wants breakfast.
—*Author unknown*

That's the only dog I know who can smell someone just *thinking* about food.

—*Charles M. Schultz, cartoonist (1922–2000)*

Many dog owners believe that as much as 60 percent of their pet's brain is set aside solely to demonstrate applications of the verb "to eat"—in both the active and passive forms.

—*Stanley Coren, psychologist and author (b. 1942)*

Every boy who has a dog should also have a mother, so the dog can be fed regularly.   —*Author unknown*

The only food he has ever stolen has been down on a coffee table. He claims that he genuinely believed it to be a table meant for dogs.

—*Jean Little, Canadian author (b. 1932)*

If you wish a dog to follow you, feed him.

—*Proverb*

A good dog deserves a good bone.

—*Ben Jonson, English playwright (1572–1637)*

> **If a dog's prayers were answered, bones would rain from the sky.**
>
> —*Turkish proverb*

A bone to the dog is not charity. Charity is the bone shared with the dog, when you are just as hungry as the dog. —*Jack London, adventurer and author (1876–1916)*

Man is an animal that makes bargains; no other animal does this—no dog exchanges bones with another.

—*Adam Smith, Scottish politician and economist (1723–1790)*

While a dog gnaws the bone, companions would be none. —*Latin proverb*

But I have always liked bird dogs better than kennel-fed dogs myself—you know, one that will get out and hunt for food rather than sit on his fanny and yell.

—*Charles E. Wilson, former president of General Motors (1890–1961)*

A hungry dog hunts best.

—*Lee Trevino, golfer (b. 1939)*

Compared to their sense of smell, dogs seem to pay a lot less attention to their sense of taste. Apparently they believe that if something fits into their mouths, then it is food, no matter what it tastes like.

—*Stanley Coren, psychologist and author (b. 1942)*

Dogfights

I'll get you, my pretty, and your little dog, too.

[*Line spoken by the witch to Dorothy in* The Wizard of Oz]

—*Noel Langley, South African writer (1911–1980)*

In the old days villains had moustaches and kicked the dog. Audiences are smarter today.

—*Alfred Hitchcock, English director (1899–1980)*

These Republican leaders have not been content with attacks on me, on my wife, or on my sons. No, not content with that, they now include my little dog, Fala. Well, of course, I don't resent attacks . . . but Fala does resent them.

[It was alleged that the president's Scottie, Fala, who was at his side everywhere, had been mistakenly left on an island off the coast of Alaska. Since it was wartime, Roosevelt's opponents said that at the cost of millions a destroyer had brought the dog home. Later the rumor proved to be unsubstantiated.]

—*Franklin D. Roosevelt, 32nd president of the United States (1882–1945)*

He that would strike my dog would strike me.

—*Scottish proverb*

While two dogs are fighting for a bone, a third runs away with it. —*Author unknown*

His bark is worse than his bite.

—*English proverb*

A dog is not considered a good dog because he is a good barker. A man is not considered a good man because he is a good talker.

—*Chuang-tzu, Chinese sage (ca. 250 B.C.)*

One barking dogs sets the street barking. —*Proverb*

Beware of a silent dog and still water. —*Latin proverb*

Cowardly dogs bark loudest.
—*John Webster, English playwright (ca. 1580–ca. 1625)*

When a dog wags his tail and barks at the same time, how do you know which end to believe?

—*Author unknown*

A barking dog never bites.   —*Author unknown*

Killing the dog does not cure the bite.

—*Abraham Lincoln, 16th president of the United States (1809–1865)*

A dog's bark may be worse than his bite, but everyone prefers his bark.   —*Author unknown*

The man recover'd of the bite, the dog it was that died.   —*Oliver Goldsmith, Irish author (1728–1774)*

Be careful, Peter is one Republican in the White House who bites.

[Warning visitors about his wire fox terrier, Peter Pan]

—Calvin Coolidge, 30th president of
the United States (1872–1933)

Better to give your path to a dog than be bitten by him in contesting for the right.

—Abraham Lincoln, 16th president of
the United States (1809–1865)

 **The dog with the bone is always in danger.**

—Author unknown

This business is dog eat dog and nobody is gonna eat me.

—Sam Goldwyn, Polish-born American
movie producer (1882–1974)

> **Revenge is often like biting a dog because the dog bit you.**
> —*Austin O'Malley, oculist (1858–1932)*

The wild boar is often held by a small dog.
—*Ovid, Roman poet (43 B.C.–A.D. 17)*

When a dog bites a man, that is not news, because it happens so often. But if a man bites a dog, that is news.
—*John B. Bogart, journalist and former editor of the* New York Sun *(1848–1921)*

Muggs was always sorry, Mother said, when he bit someone, but we could never understand how she figured this out. He didn't act sorry.
—*James Thurber, author and cartoonist (1894–1961)*

Every dog is allowed one bite, but a different view is taken of a dog that goes on biting all the time. He may not get his licence returned when it falls due.

—*Harold Wilson, English statesman (1916–1995)*

What counts is not necessarily the size of the dog in the fight but the size of the fight in the dog.

—*Dwight D. Eisenhower, 34th president of the United States and commander of the allied forces in World War II (1890–1969)*

Man he hurt me. I looked up and thought, I have to get up—my dogs would get up. I can't quit—my dogs don't quit. —*Gerald McClellan, boxer (b. 1968)*

Even the tiniest Poodle or Chihuahua is still a Wolf at heart.

—*Dorothy Hinshaw Patent, author (b. 1940)*

His puppyhood was a period of foolish rebellion. He was always worsted, but he fought back because it was his nature to fight back. And he was unconquerable.

—*Jack London, adventurer and author (1876–1916)*

A gentle hound should never play the cur.

—*John Skelton, English priest and poet (1460–1529)*

Cave Canem.
[Beware of dog]

—*Mosaic sign found in a Roman home*

It was a small town: Ferguson, Ohio. When you entered there was a big sign and it said, "Welcome to Ferguson. Beware of the Dog."

—*Jackie Vernon, actor and comedian (1925–1987)*

The disposition of noble dogs is to be gentle with people they know and the opposite with those they don't know.

—*Plato, Greek philosopher (427 B.C.–347 B.C.)*

Even the tiniest poodle is lionhearted, ready to do anything to defend home, master, and mistress.

—*Louis Sabin, author (b. 1930)*

The next-door neighbors had a German police dog that . . . acts as a bodyguard for the lady of the house and one day we was over there and the host says to slap his Mrs. on the arm and see what happened so I slapped her on the arm and I can still show you what happened.

—*Ring Lardner, author and humorist (1885–1933)*

A watchdog is a dog kept to guard the house, usually by sleeping where a burglar would awaken the household by falling over him. —*Author unknown*

I am called a dog because I fawn on those who give me anything, I yelp at those who refuse, and I set my teeth in rascals. —*Diogenes, Greek author (ca. 320 B.C.)*

A barking dog is often more useful than a sleeping lion. —*Washington Irving, author (1783–1859)*

Every dog is a lion at home.
—*Giovani Torriano, Italian writer*

They had a . . . dog called Bluey. A known psychopath, Bluey would attack himself if nothing else was available.
—*Clive James, Australian writer and broadcaster (b. 1939)*

There is one other reason for dressing well, namely that dogs respect it, and will not attack you in good clothes.

—*Ralph Waldo Emerson, essayist and poet (1803–1882)*

A dog is a dog except when he is facing you. Then he is "Mr. Dog."

—*Haitian farmer*

When a dog runs at you, whistle for him.

—*Henry David Thoreau, writer (1817–1862)*

Keep running after a dog, and he will never bite you.

—*François Rabelais, French humorist (1483–1533)*

Upon entering the little country store, the stranger noticed a sign saying "DANGER! BEWARE OF DOG!" posted on the glass door. Inside he noticed a harmless old hound dog asleep on the floor beside the cash register. He asked the store manager, "Is THAT the dog folks are supposed to beware of?" "Yep, that's him," he replied. The stranger couldn't help but be amused. "That certainly doesn't look like a dangerous dog to me. Why in the world would you post that sign?" "Because," the owner replied, "before I posted that sign, people kept tripping over him."   —*Author unknown*

3

Pedigree Pups and Mutts

Breeds and Mixed Breeds

> **If you are a police dog, where's your badge?**
>
> *[The question asked of his German shepherd]*
>
> —James Thurber, author and cartoonist
> (1894–1961)

Never have I experienced a serenity and sweetness of disposition as with my Chocolate Lab.

> —*Mortimer B. Zuckerman, Canadian-born American magazine editor and publisher (b. 1937)*

An Airedale can do anything any other dog can do and then whip the other dog if he has to.

> —*Theodore Roosevelt, 26th president of the United States (1858–1919)*

Breed a Pointer with an Irish Setter you get a Pointsetter. A traditional Christmas Pet.

> —Good Dog! *magazine*

The pug is living proof that God has a sense of humor. —*Margot Kaufman, writer*

I have a great dog. She's half Lab, half pit bull. A good combination. Sure, she might bite off my leg, but she'll bring it back to me. —*Jimi Celeste, comedian*

If a picture wasn't going very well I'd put a puppy dog in it, always a mongrel, you know, never one of the full-bred puppies. And then I'd put a bandage on its foot. . . . —*Norman Rockwell, illustrator (1894–1978)*

He likes to take strolls by himself and believes dog-catchers are friendly innkeepers who'll take care of a meal. He's gullible and has never learned to fight back against a ruthless world.

[Speaking about his Labrador retriever, which has a weight problem as well as a wandering eye]

—*Tom Hayden, political activist and former state legislator (b. 1939)*

The dog is dressed just like me at the climax of my act.

[Commenting about her Chinese Crested Dog,

which is also is known as the Chinese Naked Dog
because one of the varieties is practically furless]
—*Gypsy Rose Lee, stripper and actress (1914–1970)*

Breed a Boxer with a German Shorthaired Pointer,
you get a Boxershorts. A dog never seen in public.
—Good Dog! *magazine*

I hope if dogs ever take over the world, and they
choose a king, they don't just go by size, because I bet
there are some Chihuahuas with some good ideas.
—*"Deep Thoughts" by Jack Handey, on* Saturday Night Live

I wonder if other dogs think poodles are members of
a weird religious cult.   —*Rita Rudner, comedian (b. 1955)*

I have a rottweiler so mean, he ate the neighbor's
weenie dog. Now he's a bratweiler.
—*Nick Arnette, comedian*

A Pekinese is not a pet dog; he is an under-sized lion. —*A. A. Milne, English author (1882–1956)*

Breed a Deerhound with a terrier, you get a Derriere. True to the end! —Good Dog! *magazine*

It sometimes takes days, even weeks, before a dog's nerves tire. In the case of terriers it can run into months. —*E. B. White, author (1899–1985)*

Pomeranians speak only to Poodles and Poodles speak only to God.
—*Charles Kuralt, television journalist (1934–1997)*

A professional dog-walker was leading her charge toward the entrance to the park. A man walked up to her and said, "That's a beautiful dog. Does it have a pedigree?" She raised her eyebrows. "If this dog could talk," she said, "he wouldn't speak to either of us."

—*Author unknown*

The noblest of all dogs is the hot dog; it feeds the hand that bites it.

—*Lawrence J. Peter, Canadian author (1919–1990)*

Breed a Labrador Retriever with a Curly Coated Retriever, you get a Lab Coat Retriever. The choice for research scientists.

—Good Dog! *magazine*

Things that upset a terrier may pass virtually unnoticed by a Great Dane.

—*Smiley Blanton, author (1882–1966)*

The first one was named Max. When he died I got another, and I gave him a different name. Yet he looked like Max, and he acted like Max and sometimes I found myself calling him Max. So I said to myself, "If he wants to be Max then he is Max." . . . I suppose that I wanted Max to live with me forever. That is the nice thing about a purebred dog—if you find one that you like, they are so much the same that you can have him again and again and they need never really die. So when I get a Dachshund puppy who starts with the name Rolle or the name Jolly, I know that sooner or later they will turn into Max. That is because in their genes they are all Max, and that is who I wish to live with.

[Answering the question why he named all of his dogs Max]

—*Kurt Koffka, German founder of Gestalt psychology (1886–1941)*

A Chihuahua. They're good. If you lose one, just empty out your purse.

—*Jean Carroll, comedian*

He was an Afghan Hound named Kabul. Since him I have had other Afghan Hounds. . . . Perhaps I am looking for his ghost. He is the only one that I sometimes think about. Often, if he comes into my mind when I am working, it alters what I do. The nose on the face I am drawing gets longer and sharper. The hair of the woman I am sketching gets longer and fluffy, resting against her cheeks like his ears rested against his head.

[Responding when asked if he had a favorite dog or breed]

—*Pablo Picasso, Spanish painter and sculptor (1881–1973)*

Dachshunds are ideal dogs for small children, as they are already stretched and pulled to such a length that the child cannot do much harm one way or the other.

—*Robert Benchley, actor and author (1889–1945)*

A man once told me that his dog was half pit bull and half Poodle. He claimed that it wasn't much good as a guard dog, but it was a vicious gossip.

—*Stanley Coren, psychologist and author (b. 1942)*

Millie, the young Springer, is sitting beside me, head in my lap as I type, practicing the "spaniel gaze." At sixteen months she's already got it down. The spaniel heart is warm. The soft spaniel eye brims with love. If ever the world's diplomats and arms negotiators learn the spaniel gaze there will be peace on earth.

—*Larry Shook, pacifist, journalist, and author*

Dalmatians are not only superior to other dogs, they are like all dogs, infinitely less stupid than men.

—*Eugene O'Neill, playwright (1888–1953)*

My father was a Saint Bernard, my mother was a Collie, but I am a Presbyterian.

—*Mark Twain, author and humorist (1835–1910)*

Out of the vast sea of assorted dogs that I have had dealings with, by far the noblest, the best, and the most important was the first. . . . He was an old style collie, beautifully marked, with a blunt nose, and a great natural gentleness and intelligence.

—E. B. White, *author (1899–1985)*

Breed a Bulldog with a Shih Tzu and you get a Bull-shitz.

—Good Dog! *magazine*

Yes, he's got all them different kinds of thoroughbred blood in him, and he's got other kinds you ain't mentioned and that you ain't slick enough to see.

—Don Marquis, *author and humorist (1878–1937)*

> The Airedale . . . an unrivaled mixture of brains, and clownish wit, the very ingredients one looks for in a spouse.
>
> —*Chip Brown, journalist and writer*

It looks like a miniature hippopotamus with badly fitting panty hose all over.

[Speaking about the Chinese Shar-pei]

—*Roger Caras, author and president emeritus of the ASPCA (b. 1928)*

Newfoundland dogs are good to save children from drowning, but you must first have a pond of water handy and a child, or else there will be no profit in boarding a Newfoundland.

—*Henry Wheeler Shaw, humorist (1818–1885)*

All Dobermans should be named "Einstein." Well, perhaps that's too lavish praise. They're a bit weak on mathematics, but they certainly could earn a Ph.D. in any other subject.

—*Morton Wilson, professional dog trainer*

Of any beast, none is more faithful found
Nor yeelds more pastime in house, plaine, or woods,
Nor keepes his master's person, nor his goods,
With greater care, than doth the dog or hound.

—*Joachim Camerarius, German Lutheran theologian (1500–1574)*

Spaniels by Nature are very loving, surpassing all other Creatures, for in *Heat* and *Cold, Wet* and *Dry, Day* and *Night,* they will not forsake their *Master.*

—*Richard Blome, British publisher and cartographer (d. 1705)*

You should see my Corgis at sunset in the snow. It's their finest hour. About five o'clock they glow like copper.   —*Tasha Tudor, illustrator and writer (b. 1915)*

He wa'n't no common dog, he wa'n't no mongrel; he was a composite. A composite dog is a dog that is made up of all the valuable qualities that's in the dog breed—kind of a syndicate; and a mongrel is made up of all riffraff that's left over.

—*Mark Twain, author and humorist (1835–1910)*

I understand that most ladies tend to prefer lap dogs. . . . Perhaps I am an exception.

[On her boxer, Keeper]

—*Emily Brontë, English author (1818–1848)*

The Heimlich maneuver works on house pets. My pit bull was choking on his dinner. I squeezed his stomach and the neighbor's cat shot right out.

—*Scott Wood, comedian*

Mix a Newfoundland with a Bassett Hound, you get the Newfound Asset Hound. A dog for financial advisors.
—Good Dog! *magazine*

His herding instinct is so strong that he confuses tractors on a baseball field for sheep. He was hospitalized twice. Once by a line drive and once for attacking a tractor tread.

[Speaking about his border collie]

—*Tom Hayden, political activist and former state legislator (b. 1939)*

The Saint Bernards work best in teams of at least three dogs. They are sent out on patrols following storms, and they wander the paths looking for stranded travelers. If they come upon a victim, two dogs lie down beside the person to keep him warm; one of the two licks his face to stimulate him back to consciousness. Meanwhile, another dog will have already started back to the hospice to sound the alarm.

—*Stanley Coren, psychologist and author (b. 1942)*

The intelligence of a Poodle and the loyalty of a Lassie. The bark of a Shepherd and the heart of a Saint Bernard. The spots of a Dalmatian, the size of a Schnauzer, and the speed of a Greyhound. A genuine, All-American Mutt has it all.   —*ASPCA slogan*

The nose of the Bulldog has been slanted backwards so that he can breathe without letting go.
    —*Winston Churchill, British prime minister (1874–1965)*

Try throwing a ball just once for a dog. It would be like eating only one peanut or potato chip. Try to ignore the importuning of a Golden Retriever who has brought you his tennis ball, the greatest treasure he possesses!
        —*Roger Caras, author and president*
        emeritus of ASPCA (b. 1928)

His was the collie heritage—the stark need for comradeship coupled with the unconscious craving to be owned by man and to give his devotion to man, his god. —*Albert Payson Terhune, author (1872–1942)*

Jacob is a German Shepherd. (I have never understood why they aren't called German Sheepdogs. What do the Germans call shepherds?)
> —*Alan Coren, English writer and journalist (b. 1938)*

I'd rather have an inch of a dog than miles of pedigree.

> —*Dana Burnet, journalist and*
> *author (1888–1962)*

I like a bit of mongrel myself whether it's man or a dog; it's the best for every day.
> —*George Bernard Shaw, Irish playwright (1856–1950)*

I prefer mutts. The artificial construction of the gene pool is bad for the species as a whole. In a restricted gene pool, the defects pile up. The truly superior specimen is the outbred, not the inbred.

—*Michael Swift, scientist and author*

Among God's creatures two, the dog and the guitar, have taken all the sizes and all the shapes, in order not to be separated from the man.

—*Andres Segovia, Spanish guitarist (1894–1987)*

Hybrid vigor is an important concept in the plant world. You get this from combining the different strengths of different strains. It's the same with mutts—if you want a dog with hybrid vigor—get a mutt.   —*Mary Gallagher, author (b. 1947)*

From the dog's point of view, his master is an elongated and abnormally cunning dog.

—*Mabel Louise Robinson, author (1874–1962)*

He knew what people thought of his kind. "High Strung." "Spoiled Rotten." "French."
But in the next twenty-four hours, He's going to change all that. . . .
He's SMALL.
He's BLACK.
He's MAD AS HELL.
He's POODLE with a MOHAWK.
"You'll never call him Fifi again."

—*Lynda Barry, cartoonist (b. 1956)*

He had splendid conformation—broad shoulders, white hair and erect carriage—and was beautifully turned out in an ensemble of rich brown. One was inclined to hope he would, in the end, award first prize to himself.

[Commenting on a judge at a dog show]
—*Red Smith, journalist (1905–1982)*

4
Teaching Your Dog New Tricks

Obedience School Valedictorians and Drop-outs

The difference between "trained OK" and "trained perfectly" doesn't really matter all that much to me. I once did a film with Lassie. When that dog got excited he jumped all over Rudd Weatherwax [Lassie's trainer]. Now that's the smartest dog in the world. If the world's best-trained dog can jump around to show he's happy then my dogs should be allowed to do the same.   —*Jimmy Stewart, actor (1908–1997)*

He listens to his trainer real good. He just doesn't listen to me. I still can't get him to do nothing.

[On his Akita after the dog completed an obedience course with a professional dog trainer]

—Evander Holyfield, boxer and former
heavyweight champion (b. 1962)

The phobias I meet are very often connected with the show ring. Dogs that won't be handled by judges, men or women, and who all would be champions, according to their owners, if only they would stand still for examination—not bite the judge, or stay put on a table, or keep their tails up while being looked at, or sit in the ring.

—Barbara Woodhouse, Irish professional
dog trainer (1910–1988)

Why, that dog is practically a Phi Beta Kappa. She can sit up and beg, and she can give her paw—I don't say she will, but she can. —Dorothy Parker, writer (1893–1967)

You may have a dog that won't sit up, roll over or even cook breakfast, not because she's too stupid to learn how but because she's too smart to bother.

—*Rick Horowitz, journalist*

Dogs like to obey. It gives them security.

—*James Herriot, Scottish veterinary surgeon and author (1916–1995)*

Dogs travel hundreds of miles during their lifetime responding to such commands as "come" and "fetch."

—*Stephen Baker, Austrian-born American author (b. 1923)*

Dogs come when they are called; cats take a message and get back to you later. —*Mary Bly, author*

I named my dog "Stay" . . . so I can say, "Come here, Stay. Come here, Stay."

—*Steven Wright, Canadian comedian (b. 1955)*

[My sons] named her Bridget because that way they always had their sister, Bridget, with them. People thought we were nuts because on the phone they'd hear us say, "Bridget, sit!"

[Responding when asked about his Labrador retriever, Bridget] —*Peter Fonda, actor (b. 1939)*

My dogs have never been good at things like "sit," "stay," or even "come." I think that we've given the tourists a few laughs, especially when the dogs hit the end of their leashes hard enough to drag Gloria down the street.

[Referring to his two golden retrievers and mixed-breed dogs and his wife, Gloria]

—*Jimmy Stewart, actor (1908–1997)*

And then there's the personal question so many of Lassie's fans want to ask: Is he allowed on the furniture? Of course he is—but, then, he's the one who paid for it. —*Julia Glass, journalist*

Study hard, and you might grow up to be President. But let's face it: Even then, you'll never make as much money as your dog.

[Speaking to graduates after learning that Millie, his dog, had made $889,176 in book royalties.]
—*George Bush, 41st president of the United States (b. 1924)*

Yesterday I was a dog. Today I'm a dog. Tomorrow I'll probably still be a dog. There's just so little hope of advancement.
—*Snoopy, in* You're a Good Man, Charlie Brown *by Clark Gesner, playwright and author (b. 1938)*

My dog watches me on TV. So, if I may take this opportunity, "No! No! No!"

—*Garry Shandling, comedian (b. 1949)*

No animal should *ever* jump on the dining room furniture unless absolutely certain that he can hold his own in the conversation.

—*Fran Lebowitz, journalist and author (b. 1951)*

This past Thanksgiving, my father was at the farm, and I had all 11 dogs in the house with a father who never allowed dogs in the house. And he got up to leave the table and came back and Solomon was in his chair. And he says, "This dog is in my chair." And I said, "It's the other way around, you're sitting in his chair."

[On her American cocker spaniel Solomon and her 10 other dogs, including six golden retrievers]

—*Oprah Winfrey, television talk-show host (b. 1954)*

Guests. Guests are people who come to your home to see you whine at the table, bark loudly, jump on women wearing pantyhose, and do other tricks which you wouldn't think of doing just for the family.

[From the Doggie Dictionary]

—*Peg Kehret, author (b. 1936)*

You can't keep a good man down—or an overly affectionate dog. —*Author unknown*

As soon as I arrive at the house, Laurie starts running, hits my chest, knocks me down, and licks my face. It's become a family ritual.

[Speaking about her Welsh corgi's reaction to her return to Martha's Vineyard after spending time in New York] —*Beverly Sills, opera singer (b. 1929)*

It did not take Man long—probably not more than a hundred centuries—to discover that all the animals except the dog were impossible around the house. One has but to spend a few days with an aardvark or llama, command a water buffalo to sit up and beg or try to housebreak a moose, to perceive how wisely Man set about his process of elimination and selection.

—*James Thurber, author and cartoonist (1894–1961)*

We had a dog who was named Pushinka, who was given to my father by a Soviet official. And we trained that dog to slide down the slide we had in the back of the White House. Sliding the dog down that slide is probably my first memory.

[Because of the cold war, Pushinka was not turned over to John and Caroline until the CIA had completed X-ray tests to determine that the dog had not been implanted with a spying device.]

—*John F. Kennedy Jr., editor in chief,*
George magazine (1960–1999)

My dog can bark like a congressman, fetch like an aide, beg like a press secretary and play dead like a receptionist when the phone rings.

[Entry submitted in a contest to identify the Great American Dog on Capitol Hill]

—Gerald Solomon, congressman from New York (b. 1930)

Any time you think you have influence, try ordering around someone else's dog.

—The Cockle Bur

Just give me a comfortable couch, a dog, a good book and a woman. Then if you can get the dog to go somewhere and read the book, I might have a little fun.

—Groucho Marx, comedian (1890–1977)

Asthma doesn't seem to bother me anymore unless I'm around cigars or dogs. The thing that would bother me most would be a dog smoking a cigar.

—*Steve Allen, comedian (b. 1921)*

We are pretty sure that we and our pets share the same reality, until one day we come home to find that our wistful, intelligent friend who reminds us of our better self has decided a good way to spend the day is to open a box of Brillo pads, unravel a few, distribute some throughout the house, and eat or wear all the rest. And we shake our heads in an inability to comprehend what went wrong here.

—*Merrill Markoe, writer*

Understanding your dog and knowing how to control him, develop his potentials, and resolve behavior problems, emotional conflicts and frustrations are no less essential than love and respect.

—*Michael W. Fox, English veterinarian and author (b. 1937)*

It is a truism to say that the dog is largely what his master makes of him: he can be savage and dangerous, untrustworthy, cringing and fearful; or he can be faithful and loyal, courageous and the best of companions and allies.

—Sir Ranulph Fiennes, English explorer of both
the North and South Poles (b. 1944)

There are no wild animals till man makes them so.

—Mark Twain, author and humorist
(1835–1910)

My dog! what remedy remains,
Since, teach you all I can,
I see you, after all my pains,
So much resemble man!
[On a spaniel called Beau, killing a young bird]
—William Cowper, English poet (1731–1800)

How true it is that dogs reflect the character of their masters! A noisy, blustering windbag of a man inevitably has a dog that rushes out to roar at everything that will give ground to him. The dour chap possesses a sullen beast of kind, and your hail fellow sort of person usually owns a merry member of the tail-waggers that considers all passers-by friends.

—*Paul A. Curtis, writer (b. 1913)*

My most satisfying aspect of animal training is a very simple moment. After a show when I leave the stage door . . . and there is a crowd gathered, sometimes I hear someone say the following and it makes it all worthwhile. "How did they make that dog do that?" I smile because I am the only "they" and I do it with love.

[Speaking about how he helped a severely abused dog adopted from the pound make the transition to Sandy, appearing on Broadway in Annie]

—*William Berloni, professional dog trainer and author (b. 1956)*

Lassie looked brilliant, in part because the farm family she lived with was made up of idiots. Remember? One of them was always getting pinned under the tractor, and Lassie was always rushing back to the farmhouse to alert the other ones. She'd whimper and tug at their sleeves, and they'd always waste precious minutes saying things: "Do you think something's *wrong?* Do you think she wants us to *follow* her? What *is* it, girl?" as if this had never happened before, instead of every week. What with all the time these people spent pinned under the tractor, I don't see how they managed to grow any crops whatsoever. They probably got by on federal crop supports, which Lassie filed the applications for.　　　　—*Dave Barry, humorist (b. 1947)*

I can train any dog in five minutes. It's training the owner that takes longer.

　　　　　　　—Barbara Woodhouse, Irish professional
　　　　　　　dog trainer (1910–1988)

I was haunted by trainers going "Up, up, up, get up."
You find yourself picking your head up and then realizing, They aren't talking to me.

[Talking about the six-month film shoot in London of 101 Dalmatians*]*   —*Jeff Daniels, actor (b. 1955)*

Every dog should have a man of his own. There is nothing like a well-behaved person around the house to spread the dog's blanket for him, or bring him his supper when he comes home man-tired at night.

—*Corey Ford, humorist and author (1902–1969)*

Most owners are at length able to teach themselves to obey their dog.

—*Robert Morley, English actor and author (1908–1992)*

Hardly any animal can look as deeply disappointed as a dog to whom one says "no."

—*Jeffrey Moussaieff Masson, author (b. 1941)*

The eyes of a dog, the expression of a dog, the warmly wagging tail of a dog and the gloriously cold damp nose of a dog were in my opinion all God-given for one purpose only—to make complete fools of us human beings.

—*Barbara Woodhouse, Irish professional dog trainer (1910–1988)*

I like them all—pointers, setters, retrievers, spaniels—what have you. I've had good ones and bad of several kinds. Most of the bad ones were my fault and most of the good ones would have been good under any circumstances.

—*Gene Hill, columnist and author (1928–1997)*

There's not much you can do with a terrier, ma'am.

—*Los Angeles dog trainer*

Because of Diamond, I have had to begin much of the work afresh. I will not, however, rid myself of her, nor even punish her. She knew not what she was doing, and that which she did was for my protection and for love of my person. Her place remains at my side or against my feet when I lie abed.

[Newton's Pomeranian, Diamond, in an attempt to guard her master against a stranger at the door, accidentally knocked over a candle on his writing desk, burning all of his papers. As a result, his writings on the law of gravity were destroyed.]

—*Sir Isaac Newton, English mathematician and physicist (1642–1727)*

Intelligent dogs rarely want to please people whom they do not respect.

—*William R. Koehler, professional dog trainer (b. 1914)*

Mutts are often better to work with. Sometimes, some of the breed dogs get hyper and have lots of health problems. Mutts are just great!

[Speaking about training Maui, the collie mix who plays Murray on Mad About You]

—*Betty Linn, animal trainer*

Do not make the mistake of treating your dogs like humans or they will treat you like dogs. —*Martha Scott, English author (b. 1897)*

Men cannot think like dogs. . . . [There exists] a sharp difference in the mental capacity of humans and canines. For example, a human who is given an intricate problem will spend all day trying to solve it, but a canine will have the sense to give up and do something else instead.

—*Corey Ford, author and humorist (1902–1969)*

> The first rule in successful dog training is to be smarter than the dog. Which is why some breeds are easier to train than others.
>
> —*Author unknown*

I have a spaniel that defrocked a nun last week. He took hold of the cord. I had hold of the leash. It was like elephants holding tails. Imagine me undressing a nun, even second hand.

—*E. B. White, author (1899–1985)*

There is no such thing as a difficult dog, only an inexperienced owner.

—Barbara Woodhouse, Irish professional
dog trainer (1910–1988)

Though he had very little Latin beyond "Cave canem," he had, as a young dog, devoured Shakespeare (in a tasty leather binding).

[From 101 Dalmatians*]*

—Dodie Smith, English writer (1896–1990)

To Tom Carlson or his dog—depending on whose taste it best suits.

[The inscription Nash wrote on the second copy of one of his books for radio director Tom Carlson. The first copy was chewed up by Carlson's dog.]

—Ogden Nash, poet (1902–1971)

Home computers are being called upon to perform many new functions, including the consumption of homework formerly eaten by the dog.

—Doug Larson, columnist

I had a linguistics professor who said that it's man's ability to use language that makes him the dominant species on the planet. That may be. But I think there's one other thing that separates us from animals—we aren't afraid of vacuum cleaners.

—Jeff Stilson, comedian and comedy writer

Cat's motto: No matter what you've done wrong, always try to make it look like the dog did it.

—Author unknown

Rambunctious, rumbustious, delinquent dogs become angelic when sitting.

—Ian Dunbar, English veterinarian and author (b. 1946)

Everyone's pet is the most outstanding. This begets mutual blindness.

—Jean Cocteau, French writer and film director (1889–1963)

There is only one smartest dog in the world, and every boy has it. *—Author unknown*

No dog is as well bred or as well mannered or as distinguished and handsome.

[On his dalmatian, Blemie]

—Eugene O'Neill, playwright (1888–1953)

He had as much fun in the water as any person I have known. You didn't have to throw a stick in the water to get him to go in. Of course, he would bring back a stick to you if you did throw one in. He would even have brought back a piano if you had thrown one in.

—*James Thurber, author and cartoonist (1894–1961)*

My Labrador retriever had a nervous breakdown. I kept throwing him a boomerang.

—*Nick Arnette, comedian*

It is hard to teach an old dog new tricks.

—*William Camden, English historian (1551–1623)*

Nothing but love has made the dog lose his wild freedom, to become the servant of man.

—*D. H. Lawrence, English author (1885–1930)*

She is such a scene-stealer. She's got these lashes and big eyes, and when she walks on to the set everybody just says "ooh."

[Talking about Jill, who played the dog, Verdell, in the movie As Good As It Gets]

—Greg Kinnear, actor (b. 1967)

When I played Lady Day, I took Aba onstage with me as a joke. He started singing—in tune!—and the audience loved it.

[Responding when asked about what tricks her poodle Aba did]

—Eartha Kitt, actress and singer (b. 1927)

The dog is like a liberal. He wants to please everybody.

—William Kunstler, American attorney and radical (1919–1995)

Any member introducing a dog into the Society's premises shall be liable to a fine of one pound. Any animal leading a blind person shall be deemed to be a cat. —*Rule 46, Oxford Union Society, London*

A blind person walking down Yonge Street in Toronto commanded his dog to turn right to what he thought was the subway entrance. He had miscalculated and found himself completely disoriented in a dead-end alley. A passerby saw his dilemma and asked if he could help. "Yes, thank you," said the blind man, "I was trying to get to the subway." The man leaned over to the dog and said slowly and distinctly in the dog's ear, "TAKE . . . HIM . . . TO . . . THE . . . SUBWAY."
[Reporting story as told to him]
—*Unknown guide dog trainer*

I think animal testing is a terrible idea; they get all nervous and give the wrong answers.   —*Author unknown*

Trained or not, he'll always be his own dog to a degree.
—*Carol Lea Benjamin, professional dog trainer and author*

Humans have externalized their wisdom—stored it in museums, libraries, the expertise of the learned. Dog wisdom is inside the blood and bones.

—*Donald McCaig, author (b. 1940)*

Dogs are not people dressed up in fur coats, and to deny them their nature is to do them great harm.

—*Jeanne Schinto, writer (b. 1951)*

Humans are aware of very little, the artificial brainy side of life, the worries and bills and the mechanisms of jobs, the doltish psychologies we've placed over our lives like a stencil. A dog keeps his life simple and unadorned. He is who he is, and his only task is to assert this.

[From The Last Days of the Dog-Men*]*

—*Brad Watson, author*

If you don't want your dog to have bad breath, do what I do: Pour a little Lavoris in the toilet.

—*Jay Leno, comedian and talk-show host (b. 1950)*

All my dogs have been scamps and thieves and troublemakers and I've adored them all.

—*Helen Hayes, actress (1900–1993)*

You become responsible forever for what you have tamed.

—*Antoine de Saint-Exupéry, French author and aviator (1900–1944)*

But ask now the beasts and they shall teach thee.
—Job 12:7

The dogs in our lives, the dogs we come to love and who (we fervently believe) love us in return, offer more than fidelity, consolation, and companionship. They offer comedy, irony, wit, and a wealth of anecdotes, the "shaggy dog stories" and "stupid pet tricks" that are commonplace pleasures of life. They offer, if we are wise enough or simple enough to take it, a model for what it means to give your heart with little thought of return. Both powerfully imaginary and comfortingly real, dogs act as mirrors for our own beliefs about what would constitute a truly humane society. Perhaps it is not too late for them to teach us some new tricks.

—Marjorie Garber, author and Harvard professor

5

Making Heads or Tails of It

Communicating with Your Dog

One reason a dog is such a lovable creature is his tail wags instead of his tongue.　　　*—Author unknown*

While he has not, in my hearing, spoken the English language, he makes it perfectly plain that he understands it. And he uses his ears, tail, eyebrows, various rumbles and grumbles, the slant of his great cold nose or a succession of heartrending sighs to get his meaning across.　　　*—Jean Little, Canadian author (b. 1932)*

If dogs could talk, it would take a lot of fun out of owning one.

—*Andy Rooney, television journalist (b. 1919)*

Usually they are quick to discover that I cannot see or hear. . . . It is not training but love which impels them to break their silence about me with the thud of a tail rippling against my chair on gambols round the study, or news conveyed by expressive ear, nose, and paw. Often I yearn to give them speech, their motions are so eloquent with things they cannot say.

—*Helen Keller, author and humanitarian (1880–1968)*

If dogs could talk, perhaps we would find it as hard to get along with them as we do with people.

—*Karel Capek, Czech author (1890–1938)*

Dogs. They are better than human beings because they know but they do not tell.

—Emily Dickinson, poet and recluse (1830–1886)

The dog has an absolutely uncanny knack of knowing what we are thinking, even of what we are feeling.   —Brian Vesey-Fitzgerald, Welsh author (1900–1981)

All knowledge, the totality of all questions and answers, is contained in the dog.

—Franz Kafka, Czech author (1883–1924)

The world was conquered through the understanding of dogs; the world exists through the understanding of dogs. —*Friedrich Nietzsche, German philosopher (1844–1900)*

My Flush clearly understands articulate language. . . . 'Dinner,' 'cakes,' 'milk,' 'go downstairs,' 'go out,' everybody's name in the house, 'go & kiss Miss Barrett,' 'kiss' (abstractedly)— 'kiss the hand,' 'kiss the face,'—my Flush understands & applies all that. . . . yes, all that—and a great deal more.

[Browning tried to teach Flush, her cocker spaniel, arithmetic and reading so as to be able to play dominoes with the dog, having heard of a man reportedly doing so. The poet wanted to be able to entertain herself because she was often confined to bed due to illness.]

> —*Elizabeth Barrett Browning, English poet (1806–1861)*

Humans were denied the speech of animals. The only common ground of communication upon which dogs and men can get together is in fiction.

[From "Memoirs of Yellow Dog"]

—*O. Henry, author (1862–1910)*

Many of us have to spell words such as "out," "cookie," and "bath" when conversing with other people, lest we unnecessarily excite our pets. And even then they often understand. I've actually had clients who resorted to using a second language around their dogs, but after a while their perceptive pooches caught on. Who says dogs don't understand us?

—*Warren Eckstein, radio pet-show host*

He is so shaggy. People are amazed when he gets up and they suddenly realize they have been talking to the wrong end. —*Elizabeth Jones, Welsh author (b. 1942)*

Talking to dogs is one of the few acts of faith still made nowadays.

—*Paul Jennings, Australian children's author (b. 1943)*

The friendship of a dog is precious. It becomes even more so when one is so far removed from home. . . . I have a Scottie. In him I find consolation and diversion . . . he is the "one person" to whom I can talk without the conversation coming back to war.

—*Dwight D. Eisenhower, 34th president of the United States and commander of allied forces in World War II (1890–1969)*

When most of us talk to our dogs, we tend to forget they're not people. —*Julia Glass, journalist*

You can say any fool thing to a dog, and the dog will give you this look that says, "My God, you're RIGHT! I NEVER would have thought of that."

—*Dave Barry, humorist (b. 1947)*

Many dogs can understand almost every word humans say, while humans seldom learn to recognize more than half a dozen barks, if that. And barks are only a small part of the dog language. A wagging tail can mean so many things. Humans know that it means a dog is pleased, but not what a dog is saying about his pleasedness. (Really, it is very clever of humans to understand a wagging tail at all, as they have no tails of their own.)

[From 101 Dalmatians*]*

—*Dodie Smith, English writer (1896–1990)*

A **dog** can express more with his tail in minutes, than his **owner** can express with his tongue in hours.

—*Author unknown*

He was born in Bercy on the outskirts of Paris and trained in France, and while he knows a little Poodle-English, he responds quickly only to commands in French. Otherwise he has to translate, and that slows him down.

[Speaking about his French poodle, Charley]
—John Steinbeck, novelist (1902–1968)

An animal's eyes have the power to speak a great language.

—Martin Buber, Austrian-born Jewish theologian and philosopher (1878–1965)

They [dogs] never talk about themselves but listen to you while you talk about yourself, and keep up an appearance of being interested in the conversation.

—Jerome K. Jerome, English humorist (1859–1933)

Say something idiotic and nobody but a dog politely wags his tail.   *—Virginia Graham, author (1914–1998)*

Sometimes you panic and find yourself emitting remarks so profoundly inane that you would be embarrassed to say them to your dog. Your dog would look at you and think to itself, "I may lick myself in public, but I'd never say anything as stupid as that."

—*Dave Barry, humorist (b. 1947)*

No one appreciates the very special genius of your conversation as a dog does.

—*Christopher Morley, writer (1890–1957)*

The best thing about animals is that they don't talk much.

—*Thornton Wilder, playwright and author (1897–1975)*

I went to the cinema the other day and in the front row was an old man and with him was his dog. It was a sad funny kind of film, you know the type. In the sad part, the dog cried his eyes out, and in the funny part, the dog laughed its head off. This happened all the way through the film. After the film had ended, I decided to go and speak to the man. "That's the most amazing thing I've seen," I said. "That dog really seemed to enjoy the film." The man turned to me and said, "Yeah, it is. He hated the book."

—*Author unknown*

My neighbor has two dogs.
One of them says to the other, "Woof!"
The other replies, "Moo!"
The dog is perplexed. "'Moo'? Why did you say 'Moo'?"
The other dog says, "I'm trying to learn a foreign language."

—*Morey Amsterdam, comedian (1914–1996)*

6
For the Love of Dogs

Unashamedly Dog Lovers

> A **dog** is like an eternal Peter Pan, a child who never grows old and who therefore is always available to love and be loved.
>
> —*Aaron Katcher, educator and psychiatrist*

He cannot be a gentleman that loveth not a dog.

—*Proverb*

My dogs.

[*Responding to* Vanity Fair's *question, "Who or what is the greatest love of your life?"*]

—Bill Blass, fashion designer (b. 1922)

Who loves me will love my dog.

—Saint Bernard, French monk (1090–1153)

A lover tries to stand in well with the pet dog of the house.

—Molière, French playwright (1622–1673)

You enter into a certain amount of madness when you marry a person with pets.

—Nora Ephron, screenwriter, movie director, and author (b. 1941)

I once decided not to date a guy because he wasn't excited to meet my dog. I mean, this was like not wanting to meet my mother.

—*Bonnie Schacter, founder of the Single
Pet Owner's Society Singles Group*

The greatest love is a mother's; then comes a dog's; then a sweetheart's. —*Polish proverb*

Homer was the only person who had managed to stick it out with Rex—and Rex loved him.

[Rex Harrison's son speaking about his father's relationship with his basset hound, Homer]

I won't leave Sweden without Ted. The dog is the closest thing in the world to me.

[Explaining why he had turned down a more lucrative contract to play on a team in Scotland due to "family reasons." He would have been separated

from his dog for six months because of quarantine laws.] —Lars Karlstrand, Swedish soccer player (b. 1974)

Dogs are not our whole life, but they make our lives whole.

> —Roger Caras, author and president
> emeritus of the ASPCA (b.1928)

I'm a big man and I like big dogs. . . . The dogs kept growing until only one of us could get into the elevator. It caused enough hassles so they finally kicked me out of my apartment.

[Talking about living with his two Great Danes in New York City]

> —Wilt Chamberlain, basketball player (1936–1999)

No one can fully understand the meaning of love unless he's owned a dog. He [a dog] can show you more honest affection with a flick of his tail than a man can gather through a lifetime of handshakes.

> —Gene Hill, author and columnist (1928–1997)

Until one has loved an animal, a part of one's soul remains unawakened.

—*Anatole France, French author (1844–1924)*

It is true that whenever a person loves a dog he derives great power from it. —*Old Seneca chief*

The dog has been esteemed and loved by all the people on earth and he has deserved this affection for he renders services that have made him man's best friend.

—*Alfred Barbou, French author (1846–1907)*

I could discern clearly, even at that early age, the essential difference between people who are *kind* to dogs and people who really *love* them.

[From The Confessions of a Lost Dog]

—*Frances P. Cobbe, Irish religious writer (1822–1904)*

That was the first time I knew I loved him.

[Talking about Alec Baldwin's rescue of a dog that had been hit by a car on the freeway. The couple was driving to work when Baldwin stopped the car without hesitation and dodged oncoming traffic to rescue the limping boxer. The story has a happy ending: Baldwin and Basinger were married three  *years later, the dog was adopted by the couple, who named it Gracie, and joined their fifteen other dogs and cats.]*

—Kim Basinger, actress (b. 1953)

Do you know there is always a barrier between me and any man or woman who does not like dogs.

—Ellen Glasgow, author (1874–1975)

I have had a long unabashed love affair with dogs that stretches back to early childhood.

—*Caspar Weinberger, business executive, lawyer, and former cabinet member (b. 1917)*

I class myself with Rin Tin Tin. At the end of the Depression, people were perhaps looking for something to cheer them up. They fell in love with a dog, and with a little girl.

—*Shirley Temple, actress and diplomat (b. 1928)*

Dog lovers are a good breed themselves.

—*Gladys Taber, archaeologist and writer (1899–1980)*

It is well to love even a dog when you have the opportunity, for fear you should find nothing else worth loving.

—*Louise Honorine de Choiseul, French writer (1734–1801)*

> I like any **dog that make me look good** when it stands next to me.
>
> —*Jean Harlow, actress (1911–1937)*

Dog! When we first met on the highway of life, we came from the two poles of creation. . . . What can be the meaning of the obscure love for me that has sprung up in your heart?

—*Anatole France, French author (1844–1924)*

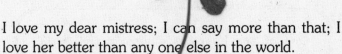

I love my dear mistress; I can say more than that; I love her better than any one else in the world.

[From Beautiful Joe, *a story told through the eyes of a dog and the first book to sell one million copies in Canada]*

—*Margaret Marshall Saunders, Canadian author (1861–1947)*

Dogs never lie about love.

Jeffrey Moussaieff Masson, author (b. 1941)

Blessed is the person who has earned the love of an old dog. —*Sidney Jeanne Seward, author (b. 1922)*

Man himself cannot express love and humility by external signs, so plainly as does a dog, when with dropping ears, hanging lips, flexuous body, and wagging tail, he meets his beloved master.

—*Charles Darwin, British naturalist (1809–1882)*

One of the happiest sights in the world comes when a lost dog is reunited with a master he loves. You just haven't seen joy till you have seen that.

—*Eldon Roark, journalist and author (1897–1979)*

Amid the cheering of the crowds, he hardly heard his master's voice, but he saw the familiar head and shoulders, and the bright flag he was waving. He raced toward the seven-foot fence; without apparent effort he rose in the air and cleared the top with a good hand-breadth to spare; then dashed up to his master that he loved, and gamboled there and licked his hand in heart-full joy. Again the victor's crown was his, and the master, a man of dogs, caressed the head of shining black with the jewel eyes of gold.

[From The Hero Dog of France]

> —Ernest Thompson Seton, English naturalist
> and writer (1860–1946)

 We give them the love we can spare, the time we can spare. In return dogs have given us their absolute all. It is without a doubt the best deal man has ever made.

> —Roger Caras, author and president
> emeritus of the ASPCA (b. 1928)

7
On the Road Again

Travels with Poochie

Charley is a mind-reading dog. There have been many trips in his lifetime, and often he has to be left at home. He knows we are going long before the suitcase has come out, and he paces and worries and whines and goes into a state of mild hysteria.

[From Travels with Charley, *the book about Steinbeck's cross-country travels with his poodle]*

—*John Steinbeck, author (1902–1968)*

I went to an exclusive kennel club. It was very exclusive. There was a sign out front: "No Dogs Allowed."

—*Phil Foster, comedian (1914–1985)*

Let's examine the dog mind: Every time you come home, he thinks it's amazing. He can't believe that you've accomplished this again. You walk in the door. The joy of it almost kills him. "He's back again! It's that guy! It's that guy!"

—*Jerry Seinfeld, comedian (b.1954)*

If you are a host to your guest, be a host to his dog also. —*Russian proverb*

I called our hotel but the response was "I'm sorry, sir. We've been booked up for months." With sudden inspiration, I called back. . . . This time I said, "Hello, this is Shana's human. . . ." and this time the response was, "Oh yes, sir. Come on down. We always have a room for you." . . . It really puts you in your place when your dog can get a hotel room, but you can't.

[As a frequent guest at a certain Holiday Inn, the staff there knew the 120-pound Great Dane (Shana) but not the dog's owner by name. Whenever Shana stayed there, crime was suddenly reduced.]

—J. Emmett Black Jr.

Mrs. Campbell once attempted to smuggle her pet Pekingese through customs by tucking him inside the upper part of her cape. "Everything was going splendidly," she later remarked, "until my bosom barked."

[From the Little Brown Book of Anecdotes]

—Beatrice Stella Campbell, English actress (1865–1940)

Like all celebrities, they've got a routine when on the road: first-class seat (always right side, second row, window), a stretch limo waiting, the finest in hotel suites and Evian water.

[About the RCA Jack Russell terriers Nipper and Chipper]   —Todd Copilevitz, journalist

I call the Crown Plaza Hotel and I say, you know, "I need a room. Do you have one?" and they say, "We don't have any rooms." I say, Well OK—I used the Oprah Winfrey thing. Now is the time to pull out the name. It's 2:30 in the morning. So I go in and I have my little doggies and the woman says to me, "I'm sorry, we don't take any dogs." By now it's 2:47. I'm in my pajamas with the dogs and I don't have a place to stay in Atlanta. So I say, "Well, do these look like dogs to you or do these look like little people with fur?" And she said they looked like dogs to her. So we were escorted out of the Crown Plaza Hotel.

[On her experience trying to get a hotel room with her two American cocker spaniels, Solomon and Sophie; the hotel has since changed their policy about dogs]

      —Oprah Winfrey, television talk-show host (b. 1954)

The Four Seasons Boston . . . in the rooms they provide their pet guests with a pet bed, dry food, and water. Also available is a special Pet Menu, which offers such items as grilled chicken and fresh corn for dogs.

—*Fran Golden, travel writer*

I've been in the hotel business over thirty years. Never yet have I called the police to eject a disorderly dog during the small hours of the night. Never yet has a dog set the bedclothes afire from smoking a cigarette. I've never found a hotel towel or blanket in a dog's suitcase, nor whiskey rings on the bureau top from a dog's bottle. Sure the dog's welcome. P.S. If he'll vouch for you, come along too.

[A reply from an American hotel manager when a vacationer wrote to ask if dogs were allowed]

—*Author unknown*

One woman very courteously approached me in a grocery store, saying, "Excuse me, but I must ask why you've brought your dog into the store." I told her that Grace is a service dog. . . . A few minutes later, she returned. "Excuse me, but you told me that your dog is allowed in the store because she's a service dog. . . . Is she Army or Navy?"   —*Terry Thistlewaite, writer*

A guy wanted to take his Chihuahua into a restaurant with him, so he put on dark glasses and "tapped" his way into the establishment.

The waiter said, "Hey! you can't bring a dog in here."

The man indignantly claimed, "I'm blind! . . . This is my Seeing Eye dog!"

"You're trying to tell me," said the waiter, "that this Chihuahua is a Seeing Eye dog?"

"What???!!" cried the man, "they gave me a Chihuahua?"   —*Author unknown*

A dog is a bond between strangers.

—*John Steinbeck, author (1902–1968)*

Where are the dogs going? you people who pay so little attention ask. They are going about their business. And they are very punctilious, without wallets, notes . . . and without brief-cases.

—*Charles Baudelaire, French poet (1821–1867)*

My Scottie refused to go for a walk with a friend of the house, but she would joyously accompany any stranger who drove a car.

—*Mazo de la Roche, Canadian author (1879–1961)*

Dogs LOVE to go for rides. A dog will happily get into any vehicle going anywhere.

—*Dave Barry, humorist (b. 1947)*

To a dog, motoring isn't just a way of getting from here to there, it's also a thrill and an adventure. The mere jingle of car keys is enough to send most any dog into a whimpering, tail-wagging frenzy.

—*Jon Winokur, author (b. 1947)*

When I started driving our old four-door green De-Soto, I always took Skip on my trips around town . . . I would get Skip to prop himself against the steering wheel, his black head peering out of the windshield, while I crouched out of sight under the dashboard. Slowing the car to ten or fifteen, I would guide the steering wheel with my right hand while Skip, with his paws, kept it steady. As we drove by the Blue Front Café, I could hear one of the men shout: "Look at that ol' dog drivin' a car!"

[From My Dog Skip]

—*Willie Morris, author, editor (1934–1999)*

Did you ever notice when you blow in a dog's face he gets mad at you? But when you take him in a car he sticks his head out the window.

—*Steve Bluestein, actor and comedian*

Better not take a dog on the space shuttle, because if he sticks his head out when you're coming home his face might burn up.

—*"Deep Thoughts" by Jack Handey on* Saturday Night Live

She never sat down in a car but stood, braced tense, facing the wind. Now and again she would turn her face toward me with an apologetic expression as though to say: "I have not forgotten that you are here but there are certain pleasures I cannot share with you." Her nose never ceased its sensitive quivering.

—*Mazo de la Roche, Canadian author (1879–1961)*

 Mutt enjoyed traveling by car, but he was an unquiet passenger. He suffered from the delusion, common to dogs and small boys, that when he was looking out the right-hand side, he was probably missing something far more interesting on the left-hand side.

—*Farley Mowat, Canadian author (b. 1921)*

I like driving around with my two dogs, especially on the freeways. I make them wear little hats so I can use the car pool lanes. —*Monica Piper, comedy writer*

Number one way life would be different if dogs ran the world: All motorists must drive with head out window.
—*David Letterman, comedian and talk-show host (b. 1947)*

She's getting quite used to jumping into limos.
—*Sue Chipperton, animal trainer of four-year-old Taco Bell commercial star, Gidget*

I've always thought a hotel ought to offer optional small animals. . . . I mean a cat to sleep on your bed at night, or a dog of some kind to act pleased when you come in. You ever notice how a hotel room feels so lifeless?
[From The Accidental Tourist]
—*Anne Tyler, author (b.1941)*

The greatest fear dogs know . . . is the fear that you will not come back when you go out the door without them.

—*Stanley Coren, psychologist and author (b. 1942)*

8

The Right Stuff

A dog's character

> A dog is not "almost human" and I
> know of no greater insult to the ca-
> nine race than to describe it as such.
>
> —*John Holmes, clergyman (1879–1964)*

The dog becomes the repository of those model human properties that we have cynically ceased to find

among humans. Where today can we find the full panoply of William Bennett's *Book of Virtues*—from Courage and Responsibility to Loyalty and Family Values—but in Lassie and Beethoven and Millie and Checkers and Spot?

—*Marjorie Garber, author and Harvard professor*

I have yet to see one completely unspoiled star, except for the animals—like Lassie.

—*Edith Head, costume designer (1898–1981)*

He may be a dog, but don't tell me he doesn't have a real grip on life.   —*Kendall Hailey, author (b. 1966)*

The more I see of men, the more I admire dogs.

—*Jeanne-Marie Roland, French revolutionary (1754–1793)*

The better I get to know men, the more I find myself loving dogs.

—*Charles de Gaulle, French former president (1890–1970)*

The average dog is a nicer person than the average person.   —*Andy Rooney, television journalist (b. 1919)*

The only one of our children who has not disillusioned us.

[On her and her husband Eugene O'Neill's dog, Blemie]

—*Carlotta O'Neill, wife of playwright Eugene O'Neill (1888–1970)*

The dog has an enviable mind. It remembers the nice things in life and quickly blots out the nasty.

—*Barbara Woodhouse, Irish professional dog trainer (1910–1988)*

To err is human: To forgive, canine.

—Author unknown

My dogs forgive anger in me, the arrogance in me, the brute in me. They forgive everything I do before I forgive myself. *—Guy de la Valdene, author*

The small percentage of dogs that bite people is monumental proof that he is the most benign, forgiving creature on earth.

—W. R. Koehler, dog trainer and author (1914–1993)

Sir, this is a unique dog. He does not live by tooth or fang. He respects the right of cats to be cats although he doesn't admire them. He turns his steps rather than disturb an earnest caterpillar. His greatest fear is that someone will point out a rabbit and suggest that he chase it. This is a dog of peace and tranquility.

—John Steinbeck, author (1902–1968)

Dogs are our link to paradise. They don't know evil or jealousy or discontent.

—*Milan Kundera, Czech author (b.1929)*

> **Dogs are the most amazing creatures; they give unconditional love. For me they are the role model for being alive.**
>
> —*Gilda Radner, comedian (1946–1989)*

If only men could love each other like dogs, the world would be a paradise.

—*James Douglas, Canadian founder of British Columbia and governor (1803–1877)*

The dog is the only thing on earth that loves you more than you love yourself.

—*Henry Wheeler Shaw, humorist (1818–1885)*

He certainly deserved the name better than those who had assumed it.

[Speaking about his dog named Duke]

—Jean-Jacques Rousseau, French revolutionary
philosopher (1712–1778)

A dog is better than I am, for he has love and does not judge.

—Abba Xanthias, monk of the Desert Fathers

When an animal has feelings that are delicate and refined, and when they can be further perfected by education, then it becomes worthy of joining human society. To the highest degree the dog has all these qualities that merit human attention.

—Count of Buffon, French naturalist
and biologist (1707–1788)

After a lifetime of affectionate regard for dogs and many years of close observation and reflection, I have reached the conclusion that dogs feel more than I do (I am not prepared to speak for other people). They feel more, and they feel more purely and more intensely. —*Jeffrey Moussaieff Masson, author (b. 1941)*

If a dog will not come to you after having looked you in the face, you should go home and examine your conscience.

—*Woodrow Wilson, 28th president of the United States (1856–1924)*

If your dog doesn't like someone you probably shouldn't either. —*Author unknown*

You really have to be some kind of a creep for a dog to reject you.

—*Joe Garagiola, baseball player and television personality (b. 1926)*

Dogs are great assets to candidates, and the feeling seems to be engendered that if a dog loves the candidate, he can't be all that bad.

Dick Gregory, activist and comedian (b. 1932)

When a man's dog turns against him it is time for his wife to pack her trunk and go home to mamma.

—*Mark Twain, author and humorist (1835–1910)*

It's funny how dogs and cats know the inside of folks better than other folks do, isn't it?

—*Eleanor H. Porter, author (1894–1961)*

The dog has seldom been successful in pulling man up to its level of sagacity, but man has frequently dragged the dog down to his.

—*James Thurber, author and cartoonist (1894–1961)*

Dogs love their friends and bite their enemies, quite unlike people, who are incapable of pure love and always have to mix love and hate in their object relations.

[Freud had a chow chow, Jo-Fi, who attended many of his therapy sessions. This was to the dismay of some of his patients, who thought the dog received more attention than they did.]

—*Sigmund Freud, Austrian founder of psychoanalysis (1856–1939)*

I love a dog. He does nothing for political reasons.   —*Will Rogers, actor and humorist (1879–1935)*

I like dogs better [than people]. They give you unconditional love. They either lick your face or bite you, but you always know where they're coming from. With people, you never know which ones will bite.

—*Greg Louganis, Olympic medalist in diving (b. 1960)*

Recollect that the Almighty, who gave the dog to be companion of our pleasures and our toils, hath invested in him with a nature noble and incapable of deceit. —*Sir Walter Scott, Scottish author (1771–1832)*

Dogs would make totally incompetent criminals. If you could somehow get a group of dogs to understand the concept of the Kennedy assassination, they would all immediately confess to it. Whereas you'll never see a cat display any kind of guilty behavior, despite the fact that several cats were seen in Dallas on the grassy knoll area, not that I wish to start rumors.

—Dave Barry, humorist (b. 1947)

I agree with Agassiz that dogs possess something very like conscience.

[Agassiz was another noted naturalist of the period] *—Charles Darwin, British naturalist (1809–1882)*

The best thing about a man is his dog.

—French proverb

The best thing about man is the dog.

—Pierre-Laurent Buyrette de Belloy, French playwright (1727–1775)

If your home burns down, rescue the dogs. At least they'll be faithful to you.   —*Lee Marvin, actor (1924–1987)*

Of the *memory* of the *dog,* and the recollection of kindness received, there are a thousand stories, from the return of Ulysses to the present day, and we have seen enough of that faithful animal to believe most of them.

—*William Youatt, veterinarian and author (1776–1847)*

 It don't care whether I'm good enough. It don't care whether I snore or not. It don't care which God I pray to. There are only three things in this world with that kind of unconditional acceptance: Dogs, donuts, and money.

[Lawrence Garfield in Other People's Money*]*
   —*Danny DeVito, actor, producer, and director (b. 1944)*

If you pick up a starving dog and make him prosperous, he will not bite you. This is the primary difference between a dog and a man.

—Mark Twain, author and humorist (1835–1910)

Gratitude: that quality which the Canine Mongrel seldom lacks; which the Human Mongrel seldom possesses! *—Lion P. S. Rees, minister*

The dog has no ambition, no self-interest, no desire for vengeance, no fear other than that of displeasing.

—Count of Buffon, French naturalist and biologist (1707–1788)

None are as fiercely loyal as dog people. In return, no doubt, for the never-ending loyalty of dogs.

—Linda Shrieves, journalist

They motivate us to play, be affectionate, seek adventure and be loyal.

> —*Tom Hayden, political activist and*
> *former state legislator (b. 1939)*

They give unconditional love and undying loyalty in return for regular meals and an occasional pat on the head. —*Jon Winokur, author (b. 1947)*

Your dog is your only philosopher.

> —*Plato, Greek philosopher (ca. 427–384)*

A dog can have a friend; he has affections and character, he can enjoy equally the field and the fireside; he dreams, he caresses, he propitiates; he offends, and is pardoned; he stands by you in adversity; he is a good fellow.

> —*Leigh Hunt, English poet and essayist (1784–1859)*

Living with a dog is easy—like living with an idealist.

—*H. L. Mencken, editor and author (1880–1956)*

A dog barks when his master is attacked. I would be a coward if I saw that God's truth is attacked and yet would remain silent.

—*John Calvin, French theologian and Protestant reformer (1509–1564)*

My dog does have his failings, of course. He's afraid of firecrackers and hides in the clothes closet whenever we run the vacuum cleaner, but, unlike me he's not afraid of what other people think of him or anxious about his public image.

—*Gary Kowalski, minister and author*

God give to me by your grace what you give to dogs by nature.

—*Mechtilda of Magdeberg, German hermit and author (1207–1282)*

Lord . . . No one but you and I understands what faithfulness is. . . . Do not let me die until, for them, all danger is driven away.

[From "The Prayer of the Dog"]

—*Carmon Bernos de Gaesztold, French religious author*

The dog was cold and in pain. But being only a dog it did not occur to him to trot off home to the comfort of the library fire and leave his master to fend for himself.

—*Albert Payson Terhune, author (1872–1942)*

Here, Gentlemen, a dog teaches us a lesson in humanity.

[While standing on the deck of a ship that was leaving the harbor, Napoleon slipped and fell overboard. He did not know how to swim and was struggling to stay afloat. A Newfoundland, seeing this from shore, swam to Napoleon and kept his head above water until the ship could make its turn and successfully rescue him.]

—*Napoleon Bonaparte, French emperor and military strategist (1769–1821)*

I know that I have had friends who would never have vexed or betrayed me, if they had walked on all fours.

—*Horace Walpole, 4th Earl of Orford, British historian and author (1717–1797)*

Only my dogs will not betray me.

—*Maria Callas, opera singer (1923–1977)*

Histories are more full of examples of the fidelity of dog than of friends.

—*Alexander Pope, English poet (1688–1744)*

A dog, I will maintain, is a very tolerable judge of beauty, as appears from the fact that any liberally educated dog does, in a general way, prefer a woman to a man.   —*Frances Thompson, Canadian author (b. 1906)*

There is no faith which has never yet been broken, except that of a truly faithful dog.

—*Konrad Z. Lorenz, Austrian naturalist (1903–1989)*

If you can resist treating a rich friend better than a
   poor friend,
If you can face the world without lies and deceit,
If you can say honestly that deep in your heart you
   have no prejudice against creed, color, religion or
   politics,
Then, my friend, you are almost as good as your
   dog.   —*Author unknown*

9
Best of Friends

A Friend to the End

God made the earth, the sky and the water, the moon and the sun. He made man and bird and beast. But He didn't make the dog. He already had one.

—*Native American saying*

We are alone, absolutely alone on this chance planet; amid all the forms of life that surround us, not one, excepting the dog, has made an alliance with us.

—*Maurice Maeterlinck, Belgian naturalist and poet (1862–1949)*

It has been 20,000 years since man and dog formed their partnership.

—*Donald McCaig, author (b. 1940)*

Stick around any place long enough and chances are you'll be taken for granted. Hang around for 20,000 years wagging your tail and being man's (and woman's) best friend, and you'll be taken for granted big time.

—*Lynn Van Matre, journalist*

His name is not wild dog anymore, but the first friend, because he will be our friend for always and always and always.

—*Rudyard Kipling, Indian-born British author (1865–1936)*

One of the most enduring friendships in history—
dogs and their people, people and their dogs.

—Terry Kay, author (b.1938)

Isn't it wonderful how dogs can win friends and influence people without ever reading a book.

—E. C. McKenzie, Australian author (b. 1902)

Gangster is the truest friend I can ever ask for.
[On his boxer, Gangster]

—Sylvester Stallone, actor and director (b. 1946)

When a man's best friend is his dog, that dog has a problem.

—Edward Abbey, writer and conservationist (1927–1989)

A species so intimately involved with our own, which has shared our life since time immemorial.

—Alfred Barbou, French author (1846–1907)

Hills—Sir—and the Sundown—and a Dog—large as myself, that my Father bought me.

[When an acquaintance asked in a letter "Who are your companions?" Dickinson wrote back and provided the above response. In 1862, Dickinson went into reclusion at the age of 32 for the remainder of her life, preferring the company of her dog, a Newfoundland, to humans.]

—Emily Dickinson, poet and recluse (1830–1886)

Extraordinary creature! So close a friend, and yet so remote.

—Thomas Mann, German author and critic (1875–1955)

Our perfect companions never have fewer than four feet.   —Colette, French author (1873–1954)

Any woman who does not thoroughly enjoy tramping across the country on a clear frosty morning with a good gun and a pair of dogs does not know how to enjoy life.

—*Annie Oakley, sharpshooter and vaudevillian (1860–1926)*

She has never messed up a single take yet. Recently I was in a scene and there was a table covered with a cloth. When the director said cut, I saw a little black nose and two paws inching out from under the cloth. She had hidden there without making a sound until we were done with the scene. She wanted to be nearer to me.

[On his poodle, Chloe, who always accompanies him to the movie set] —*Jack Lemmon, actor (b. 1925)*

To a man the greatest blessing is individual liberty; to a dog it is the last word in despair.

—*William Lyon Phelps, educator (1865–1943)*

Dog is the only animal in the world who ostensibly likes another breed better than his own. Man.

—*Ted Patrick, author*

Right now Jack lives with me. Jack is my Jack Russell. I also have a Yorkie named Ginger, but Jack and Ginger can't be in the  same place at the same time because she is very jealous. Even if Jack's not in the same state, she would growl if she heard his name.

—*Mariah Carey, singer (b. 1970)*

Nature teaches beasts to know their friends.

—*William Shakespeare, English playwright and poet (1564–1616)*

No animal I know of can consistently be more of a friend and companion than a dog.

—*Stanley Leinwoll, author*

There are two kinds of fidelity, that of dogs and that of cats: you, gentlemen, have the fidelity of cats who never leave the house.

[Speaking to French courtiers who had not followed him there, after he had escaped from Elba]

—Napoleon Bonaparte, French emperor and military strategist (1769–1821)

I can still see my first dog. . . . For six years he met me at the same place after school and convoyed me home—a service he thought up himself. A boy doesn't forget that sort of association.

—E. B. White, author (1899–1985)

Dogs love company. They place it first in their short list of needs.

—J. R. Ackerley, English writer (1896–1967)

A man and his dog is a sacred relationship. What nature hath put together let no woman put asunder.

—A. R. Gurney, playwright (b. 1930)

Outside of a dog, a book is man's best friend. Inside of a dog, it's too dark to read.

—Groucho Marx, comedian (1890–1977)

If you eliminate smoking and gambling you will be amazed to find that almost all an Englishman's pleasures can be, and mostly are, shared by his dog.

—Geroge Bernard Shaw, Irish playwright and socialist (1856–1950)

One evening at Chequers the film was *Oliver Twist*. Rufus [Churchill's poodle], as usual, had the best seat in the house, on his master's lap. At the point when Bill Sikes was about to drown his dog to put the police off his track, Churchill covered Rufus's eyes with his hand. He said, "Don't look now, dear. I'll tell you about it afterwards."

[From The Little Brown Book of Anecdotes*]*

—*Winston Churchill, British statesman,
and prime minister (1874–1965)*

Inside every Newfoundland, Boxer, Elkhound and Great Dane is a puppy longing to climb on to your lap.   —*Helen Thomson, English writer*

If a dog jumps in your lap, it is because he is fond of you; but if a cat does the same thing, it is because your lap is warmer.

—*Alfred North Whitehead, English mathematician,
philosopher, and Harvard professor (1861–1947)*

I can't think of anything that brings me closer to tears than when my old dog—completely exhausted after a hard day in the field—limps away from her nice spot in front of the fire and comes over to where I'm sitting and puts her head in my lap, a paw over my knee, and closes her eyes, and goes back to sleep. I don't know what I've done to deserve that kind of friend.

—*Gene Hill, columnist and author (1928–1997)*

He never makes it his business to inquire whether you are in the right or wrong, never bothers as to whether you are going up or down life's ladder, never asks whether you are rich or poor, silly or wise, sinner or saint. You are his pal. That is enough for him.

—*Jerome K. Jerome, English writer (1859–1927)*

If you want a friend in Washington, get a dog.

—*Harry S Truman, 33rd president of the United States (1884–1972)*

Leave it be. . . . If it came to a choice of who would have to go, you would be packing to leave, not Charlie.

[Advice given by an unknown supervisor to an employee at the White House who complained that JFK's Welsh terrier, Charlie, had bitten him]
—*Traphes Bryant, White House kennel keeper*

The poor dog, in life the firmest friend,
The first to welcome, foremost to defend.
—*Lord Byron, British poet (1788–1824)*

One reason a dog can be such a comfort when you're feeling blue is that he doesn't try to find out why. —*Author unknown*

A study conducted by the State University of New York at Buffalo Medical School suggested that in times of stress a dog is likely to be more help in calming you down than a spouse or partner. . . . Most dog owners can guess the reason why: dogs never judge us and never compete with us.

—*Marjorie Garber, author and Harvard professor*

Animals are such agreeable friends; they ask no questions; pass no criticisms.

—*George Eliot, English author (1819–1880)*

I've seen a look in dogs' eyes, a quickly vanishing look of amazed contempt, and I am convinced that basically dogs think humans are nuts.

—*John Steinbeck, author (1902–1968)*

There is no psychiatrist in the world like a puppy licking your face.

—*Bern Williams, English philosopher and Oxford professor (b. 1929)*

Everyone needs a spiritual guide: a minister, rabbi, counselor, wise friend, or therapist. My own wise friend is my dog.

—*Gary Kowalski, minister and author*

I was there in Jack Kennedy's office that day. Everything was in an uproar. I was ten feet from Kennedy's desk as Pierre Salinger [the press secretary] ran around the office taking messages and issuing orders while the President sat looking awfully worried. There was talk about the Russian fleet coming in and our fleet blocking them off. It looked like war. Out of the blue, Kennedy suddenly called for Charlie to be brought to his office.

[Charlie, the President's Welsh terrier, was Kennedy's favorite dog. Here the White House kennel keeper describes the events in the Oval Office during the Cuban missile crisis and Kennedy's order to fetch Charlie. After petting the dog for a while, the president seemed more relaxed and then asked the kennel

keeper to take Charlie back out. Kennedy then said, "I suppose that it's time to make some decisions."]
—Traphes Bryant, White House kennel keeper

Ladies and gentlemen are permitted to have friends in the kennel but not in the kitchen.
—*George Bernard Shaw, Irish playwright and socialist (1856–1950)*

When you feel lousy, puppy therapy is indicated.
—*Sara Paretsky, author (b. 1947)*

His ears were often the first thing to catch my tears. *[Speaking about her cocker spaniel, Flush]*
—*Elizabeth Barrett Browning, English poet (1806–1861)*

I have found that when you are deeply troubled, there are things you get from the silent devoted companionship of a dog that you can get from no other source. —*Doris Day, actress (b. 1924)*

With an endless assortment of children and animals living under one roof, there was always some absurd crisis that gave comic relief to my problems.
—*Sally Jessy Raphael, talk-show host (b. 1943)*

 The psychological and moral comfort of a presence at once humble and understanding—this is the greatest benefit that the dog has bestowed upon man.
—*Percy Bysshe Shelley, British poet (1792–1822)*

Thomas A. Edison was once reluctantly persuaded by his wife to attend one of the big social functions of the season in New York. At last the inventor managed to escape the crowd of people vying for his attention, and sat alone unnoticed in a corner. Edison kept looking at his watch with a resigned expression on his face. A friend edged near to him unnoticed and heard the inventor mutter to himself with a sigh, "If there were only a dog here!" —*Edmund Fuller, author*

There's just something about dogs that makes you feel good. You come home; they're thrilled to see you. They're good for the ego.

—*Janet Schulman, author (b. 1933)*

It is scarcely possible to doubt that the love of man has become instinctive in the dog.

—*Charles Darwin, British naturalist (1809–1882)*

For a man living alone dogs are almost more important than human beings.

—*Richard Katz, author and editor*

To his dog, every man is Napoleon; hence the constant popularity of dogs.

—*Aldous Huxley, English author (1894–1963)*

In order to keep a true perspective of one's importance, everyone should have a dog that will worship him and a cat that will ignore him.

—*Dereke Bruce, writer*

He is your friend, your partner, your defender, your dog. You are his life, his love, his leader. He will be yours, faithful and true, to the last beat of his heart. You owe it to him to be worthy of such devotion.

—*Author unknown*

> **The average dog has one request to all humankind. Love me.**
>
> —*Helen Exley, English editor and publisher*

I petted [Old Yeller] and made over him till he was wiggling all over to show how happy he was. I felt mean about how I'd treated him and did everything I could to let him know. . . . And that night after dark, when he sneaked into bed with me and Little Arliss, I let him sleep there and never said a word about it to Mama.
[From Old Yeller]

—*Fred Gipson, author (1908–1973)*

Hear our humble prayer, O God. . . . Make us, ourselves, to be true friends to the animals.

—*Albert Schweitzer, French missionary, philosopher, and physician (1875–1965)*

Properly trained, a man can be dog's best friend. —*Corey Ford, humorist and author (1902–1969)*

Dogs are, after all, man's best friend. The least we can do is try to understand them a little better.

—*Nicholas Dodman, veterinarian and professor*

Don't accept your dog's admiration as conclusive evidence that you are wonderful.

—*Ann Landers, advice columnist (b. 1918)*

I hope to be the kind of person my dog thinks I am.

—*Author unknown*

Folk will know how large your soul is, by the way you treat a dog!

—*Charles F. Doran, author (b. 1943)*

If you have men who will exclude any of God's creatures from the shelter of compassion and pity, you will
have men who will deal likewise with their fellow man.

*—Saint Francis of Assisi, Italian founder of the Franciscan
order and patron saint of animals (1181–1226)*

I care not for a man's religion whose dog and cat are
not the better for it.

*—Abraham Lincoln, 16th president of the
United States (1809–1865)*

The real platform for religion is based on the concepts
of compassion, respect and consideration, not just for
human beings, but for all forms of life.

—Paul Irwin, president of the Humane Society

Our task must be to free ourselves . . . by widening
our circle of compassion to embrace all living creatures and the whole of nature and its beauty.

*—Albert Einstein, German-born American
physicist (1879–1955)*

I don't believe in the concept of hell, but if I did I would think of it as filled with people who were cruel to animals. —*Gary Larson, cartoonist (b. 1950)*

The greatness of a nation and its moral progress can be judged by the way its animals are treated.

—*Mohandas Gandhi, Indian ascetic and nationalist leader (1869–1948)*

If a man be great even his dog will wear a proud look.

—*Japanese proverb*

Old age means realizing you will never own all the dogs you wanted to. —*Joe Gores, author (b. 1931)*

In dogs years, I'm dead.   —*Author unknown*

The bond with a true dog is as lasting as the ties of this earth can ever be.

> —*Konrad A. Lorenz, Austrian naturalist (1903–1989)*

Dogs don't know about beginnings, and they don't speculate on matters that occurred before their time. Dogs also don't know—or at least don't accept—the concept of death. . . . With no concept of beginnings or endings dogs probably don't know that for people, having a dog as a life companion provides a streak of light between two eternities of darkness.

> —*Stanley Coren, psychologist and author (b. 1942)*

Unmissed but by his dogs and by his groom.

> —*William Cowper, English poet (1731–1800)*

I know well enough that there have been dogs so loving that they have thrown themselves into the same grave with the dead bodies of their masters; others have stayed upon their masters' graves without stirring a moment from them, and have voluntarily starved themselves to death, refusing to touch the food that was brought them.

—*Miguel de Cervantes, Spanish author (1547–1616)*

Of all the animals, surely the dog is the only one that really shares our life, helps in our work, and has a place in our recreation. It is the only one that becomes so fond of us that sometimes it cannot go on living after its master dies. —*Fernand Mercy, writer*

This soldier, I realized, must have had friends at home and in his regiment; yet he lay there deserted by all except his dog. . . . I looked on, unmoved, at battles which decided the future of nations. Tearless, I had given orders which brought death to thousands. Yet here I was stirred, profoundly stirred, stirred to tears. And by what? By the grief of one dog.

[*Surveying the moonlit field at the end of battle, Napoleon came upon a dog sitting beside the body of his fallen master, licking his face and howling. This image continued to haunt him until his own death.*]

—*Napoleon Bonaparte, French emperor and military strategist (1769–1821)*

The dog without his master was . . . like a body without a soul.

—*Mary E. Wilkins Freeman, author (1852–1930)*

Oh the saddest of sights in a world of sin
Is the little lost pup with his tail tucked in.

—*Arthur Guiterman, poet (1871–1943)*

Why is it that my heart is so touched whenever I meet a dog lost in our noisy streets? Why do I feel such anguished pity when I see one of these creatures coming and going, sniffing everyone, frightened, despairing of ever finding its master?

—Émile Zola, French author (1840–1902)

Many people have heard the remarkable example of devotion involving a Skye terrier dog who worked for a Scottish shepherd named Old Jock. In 1858, the day after Jock was buried (with almost nobody present to mourn him except his shaggy dog) in the churchyard at Greyfriars Abbey in Edinburgh, Bobby was found sleeping on his master's grave, where he continued to sleep every night for fourteen years.

—Jeffrey Moussaieff Masson, author (b. 1941)

The dog is the most faithful of animals and would be much esteemed were it not so common. Our Lord God has made his greatest gifts the commonest.

—Martin Luther, German theologian (1483–1546)

Gentlemen of the jury: The best friend a man has in this world may turn against him and become his enemy. His son or daughter whom he has reared with loving care may prove ungrateful. . . . The one absolutely unselfish friend that man can have in this selfish world—the one that never deserts him, the one that never proves ungrateful or treacherous—is his dog. . . . He will kiss the hand that has no food to offer. . . . When all other friends desert, he remains. When riches take wings and reputation falls to pieces, he is as constant in his love as the sun in its journey through the heavens. If fortune drives the master forth an outcast in the world, friendless and homeless, the faithful dog asks no higher privilege than that of accompanying him, to guard against danger, to fight against his enemies. And when the last scene of all comes, and death takes the master in its embrace and his body is laid away in the cold ground, no matter if all other friends pursue their way, there by his graveside will the noble dog be found, his head beneath his paws, his eyes sad, but open in alert watchfulness, faithful and true even to death.

[Excerpts from the "Eulogy on the Dog" speech. This speech was given while Vest was representing a man who sued another for the killing of his dog, Drum. The trial took place in a small Missouri town. According to the recollection of Thomas T. Crittenden, counsel for the defendant and later governor of Missouri, "It was as perfect a piece of oratory as was ever heard. . . . Court, jury, lawyers, and audience were entranced. I looked at the jury and saw all were in tears." Vest won the case and the jury awarded his client $500, which was in excess of the maximum allowable damages of $150. Vest was later elected to the U.S. Senate.]

—George Graham Vest, attorney and
U.S. Senator (1830–1904)

10
Saying Good-bye

Going to Dog Heaven

When I got him out he was near froze solid and shivering. He was shaking so hard that I wasted half a glass of whiskey trying to aim it for his mouth. Must have got enough of it into him, though, since it did seem to bring him back to life.

[After saving his dog from a river when he fell through thin ice]

—*Abraham Lincoln, 16th president of the United States (1809–1865)*

The . . . dog was the only intelligent member of the family. He died a few years later. He was poisoned, and no one will convince me it wasn't suicide.

—I'm Sorry I'll Read That Again, *BBC Radio*

Jesse has a new dog. You may have noticed that his former pets have been peculiarly unfortunate. When this dog dies every employee in the White House will be at once discharged.

[Statement made to the White House staff when his son got a Newfoundland pup and after his son's other dogs had died mysteriously]

—*Ulysses S. Grant, 18th president of the United States (1822–1885)*

> **Old dogs, like old shoes, are comfortable. They might be a bit out of shape and a little worn around the edges, but they fit well.**
>
> —Bonnie Wilcox, veterinarian and author

The old dog barks backward without getting up.
I can remember when he was a pup.

—Robert Frost, poet (1874–1963)

There are three faithful friends—an old wife, an old dog, and ready money.

—Ben Franklin, statesman (1706–1790)

My dear old dog, most constant of all friends.

—William Croswell Doane, Episcopal bishop (1832–1913)

When the dog was created, it licked the hand of God and God stroked its head, saying, "What do you want, dog?" It replied, "My Lord, I want to stay with you, in heaven, on a mat in front of the gate. . . ."

—*Marie Noel, French writer (1883–1967)*

Any of us who has owned a dog that has taken particular hold on our heart has dwelt on the unfairness of allocated time. It seems but an instant . . . and the puppy we so carefully carried home and placed on the rug by our bed has suddenly become a little dim of eye, a touch slow to get up in the morning, and more and more content to lay in some sunny spot and salute our passings-by with a turning of the head and wagging of the tail. Somehow even through the dozen dogs I've owned I never cease to be surprised and a little hurt to discover that today Tippy or Ben or Judy doesn't race to the door to go out but stands in the warmth of the kitchen and merely follows me with eyes and heart.

—*Gene Hill, columnist and author (1928–1997)*

Dogs' lives are too short. Their only fault, really. —*Agnes Sligh Turnbull, author (1888–1982)*

If you have a dog, you will most likely outlive it; to get a dog is to open yourself to profound joy and, prospectively, to equally profound sadness.

—*Marjorie Garber, author and Harvard professor*

There is sorrow enough in the natural way
From men and women to fill our day;
But when we are certain of sorrow in store
Why do we always arrange for more?

—*Rudyard Kipling, Indian-born British author (1865–1936)*

I have sometimes thought of the final cause of dogs having such short lives and I am quite satisfied it is in compassion to the human race; for if we suffer so much in losing a dog after an acquaintance of ten or twelve years, what would it be if they were to live double that time?

—*Sir Walter Scott, Scottish author (1771–1832)*

I guess you don't really own a dog, you rent them, and you have to be thankful that you had a long lease.

—*Joe Garagiola, baseball player and*
television personality (b. 1926)

She died as she had been born and as she had lived, in my care, and surrounded by those who loved her.

—*Vicki W. Fowler, veterinarian*

 No louder shrieks to pitying heaven are cast, when husbands or lap-dogs breathe their last.

—*Alexander Pope, English poet*
and satirist (1688–1744)

Animals have these advantages over man: They have no theologians to instruct them, their funerals cost them nothing, and no one starts lawsuits over their wills. —*Voltaire, French philosopher and author (1694–1778)*

I feel about my dogs now, and all the dogs I had prior to this, the way I feel about children—they are that important to me. When I have lost a dog I have gone into a mourning period that lasted for months.

—*Mary Tyler Moore, actress (b. 1936)*

Two days ago we waded through the mud out to his grave beneath the pines at the foot of the hill to place a Christmas wreath on it, hoping he would look down from the Paradise of Ten Billion Trees and Unrationable Dog Biscuits and pity us.

[Speaking about his dalmatian, Blemie]

—*Eugene O'Neill, playwright (1888–1953)*

Near this spot are deposited the remains of one who possessed Beauty without Vanity, Strength without Insolence, Courage without Ferocity, and all the Virtues of Man, without his Vices. This Praise, which would be unmeaning Flattery, if inscribed over human ashes, is but a just tribute to the Memory of Boatswain, a Dog.

[Inscription on the monument to Boatswain,

Lord Byron's beloved Newfoundland dog, buried at Newstead Abbey in Nottinghamshire. The poet at one time intended to be buried in the same vault as his dog. The quote is often attributed to Byron, but it was actually written by his friend Hobhouse.]

—John Cam Hobhouse, British statesman (1786–1869)

Here Shock, the pride of all his kind, is laid,
Who fawned like man, but ne'er like man betrayed.

—John Gay, English poet (1685–1732)

> Greyfriars Bobby.
> Died 14th Jan 1872.
> Aged 16 years.
> Let his loyalty & devotion
> Be a lesson to us all.
>
> *[Inscription on a stone marking the grave of Bobby, a Skye terrier, in the church cemetery in Greyfriars, Scotland. American donors erected it in the 1930s to pay tribute to the dog that slept on his master's grave every night for fourteen years until his own death in 1872.]* —Author unknown

Foxes, rejoice! Here buried lies your foe.
  [Inscription on a stone in the wall of Euston Park, England, in memory of a hound]

—Author unknown

I cannot believe Earl Spencer could be so heartless as to bury his sister in a dog burial ground. It is a desecration.

[Statement made by a former housekeeper for the Spencer family, who says the land that Princess Diana is buried on was known to the family as "Dog Island," because that was where they buried the family pets]

At thieves, I bark'd, at lovers wagg'd my tail,
And thus I pleased both Lord and Lady Frail.
[Epitaph on the lap-dog of Lady Frail]
—*John Wilkes, English political reformer (1727–1797)*

**Here lies DASH, the Favourite Spaniel of Queen Victoria
By whose command this Memorial was Erected.
He died on the 20 December, 1840 in his 9th year.
His attachment was without selfishness,
His playfulness without malice,**

His fidelity without deceit.
**READER, if you would live beloved and die
  regretted, profit by the example of DASH.**
*[Epitaph on the gravestone of Queen Victoria's
dog, a King Charles cavalier spaniel, Dash. The dog
was buried in the castle's garden.]*

—Queen Victoria, British royalty (1819–1901)

The stone tells that it covers the white Maltese
dog. . . . They called him Bull while he still lived, but
now the silent paths of night possess his voice.
[From "Epitaph for a Dog"]

—William Tymmes, English minister (d. 1556)

His friends he loved. His direst earthly foes—
Cats—I believe he did but feign to hate.
My hand will miss the insinuated nose,
Mine eyes the tail that wagged contempt at Fate.
[An epitaph]

—Sir William Watson, English poet (1858–1935)

To mark a friend's remains
these stones arise
I never knew but one—
and here he lies.

—*Lord Byron, English poet (1788–1824)*

It is a terrible thing for an old woman to outlive her dogs.   —*Tennessee Williams, playwright (1911–1983)*

I didn't know if there was a special dog that she was looking for . . . she just slowly walked through the little burial plot, reading the names and pausing now and then to stop by a gravestone. She stooped down once to touch one of the grave markers and to brush something off of it. She looked sad and thoughtful, and finally left, without saying a word.

[Unknown member of the royal household talks about Queen Elizabeth's visit to the canine cemetery, where her dogs are buried on the castle grounds]

Major
Born a dog
Died a gentleman.

  [Epitaph on a dog's grave in Maryland]

—*Author unknown*

Brothers and Sisters, I bid you beware
Of giving your heart to a dog to tear.

—*Rudyard Kipling, Indian-born British author (1865–1936)*

In his grief over the loss of a dog, a little boy stands for the first time on tiptoe, peering into the rueful morrow of manhood. After this most inconsolable of sorrows there is nothing life can do to him that he will not be able somehow to bear.

—*James Thurber, author and cartoonist (1894–1961)*

Unlike some people who have experienced the loss of an animal, I did not believe, even for a moment, that I would never get another. I did know full well that there were just too many animals out there in need of homes for me to take what I have always regarded as the self-indulgent road of saying the heartbreak of the loss of an animal was too much ever to want to go through with it again. To me, such an admission brought up the far more powerful admission that all the wonderful times you had with your animal were not worth the unhappiness at the end.

> —*Cleveland Amory, author and animal-rights activist (1917–1998)*

My friendship with Mitzi was like the friendship that many children have with their pets. My mother and father thought it was "good for me" to have a dog for a companion. Well, it *was* good for me, but it was only many years after she died that I began to understand how good it was . . . and why.

> —*Fred Rogers, host of* Mister Rogers' Neighborhood *(b. 1928)*

The dog of your boyhood teaches you a great deal about friendship, and love, and death: Old Skip was my brother. They had buried him under our elm tree, they said—yet this was not totally true. For he really lay buried in my heart.

[From My Dog Skip*]*

—*Willie Morris, author and editor (1934–1999)*

To call him a dog hardly seems to do him justice, though inasmuch as he had four legs, a tail, and barked, I admit he was, to all outward appearances. But to those who knew him well, he was a perfect gentleman.

—*Hermione Gingold, English actress and comedian (1897–1987)*

Leave your dog outside. Heaven goes by favor. If it went by merit you would stay out and the dog would go in. —*Mark Twain, author and humorist (1835–1910)*

The sweetness of his disposition and endearing qualities are sufficiently attested by the fact, that to the last,

when sometimes his sickness en-
tailed additional and disagreeable
duties in regard to him, not a servant would hear to his days being
shortened, and when he died there
were those of the household who felt that though but a
dog he had qualities which would have adorned a
Christian. —*Charles W. Shimmain, writer*

Our German forefathers had a very kind religion.
They believed that, after death, they would meet
again all the good dogs that had been their companions in life. I wish I could believe that too.

—*Otto von Bismarck, first chancellor of
German Empire (1815–1898)*

But thinks, admitted to that equal sky, His faithful dog
shall bear him company.

—*Alexander Pope, English poet and satirist (1688–1744)*

For those who love dogs, it would be the worst form of a lie to call any place where dogs were banned "Paradise." Certainly no loving God would separate people from their canine friends for eternity.

—*Stanley Coren, psychologist and author (b. 1942)*

Shall we, because we walk on our hind feet, assume to ourselves only the privilege of imperishability?

—*George Eliot, English author (1819–1880)*

I have always felt it was human arrogance that assumes that only people have souls.

—*Anne Raver, journalist*

Be comforted, little dog, thou too in the Resurrection shall have a tail of gold.

—*Martin Luther, German theologian (1438–1546)*

If I have any beliefs about immortality, it is that certain dogs I have known will go to heaven, and very, very few persons.

—*James Thurber, author and cartoonist (1894–1961)*

You think **dogs** will not be in heaven? I tell you, they will be there before any of us.

—*Robert Louis Stevenson, Scottish author (1850–1894)*

He deserves paradise who makes his companions laugh. —*the Koran*

God turns clouds inside out to make fluffy beds for the dogs in Dog Heaven, and when they are tired from running and barking and eating ham-sandwich biscuits, the dogs find a cloud bed for sleeping. . . . God watches over each one of them. And there are no bad dreams. —*Cynthia Rylant, children's writer (b. 1954)*

How often do angels kiss our dogs? Just count the pink spots on each nose. —*Mary Clare Goodyear, writer*

The dog is a gentleman; I hope to go to his heaven, not man's. —*Mark Twain, author and humorist (1835–1910)*

If my dog is barred by the heavenly guard
We'll both of us brave the heat!
—*W. Dayton Wedgefarth, writer*

There is another world for all that live and move—a better one!
[On the death of a favorite spaniel]
—*Robert Southey, English author (1774–1843)*

At one time a synod of the Catholic Church was held in which the question of whether or not animals had a soul was discussed very seriously: would good dogs go to paradise and bad ones, who stole slices of lamb, burn in hell eternally. The denial of the soul was voted: it is enough for the honor of the species that the question was posed.

—*Alfred Barbou, French author (1846–1907)*

If there are no dogs in Heaven, then when I die I want to go where they went.

—*Author unknown*

If there is no God for thee
Then there is no God for me.

—*Anna Hempstead Branch, poet (1875–1937)*

If there is a heaven, it's certain our animals are to be there. Their lives became so interwoven with our own, it would take more than an archangel to detangle them. —*Pam Brown, English author (b. 1924)*

I explained it to St. Peter,
I'd rather stay here
Outside the pearly gate.
I won't be a nuisance,
I won't even bark, I'll be very patient and wait,
I'll be here, chewing on a celestial bone,
No matter how long you may be.
I'd miss you so much, if I went in alone,
It wouldn't be heaven for me.

—*Author unknown*

I think God will have prepared everything for our perfect happiness [in Heaven]. If it takes my dog being
there, I believe he'll be there.

—*Rev. Billy Graham, evangelist (b. 1918)*

Not the least hard thing to bear when they go from us,
these quiet friends, is that they carry away with them
so many years of our own lives.

—*John Galsworthy, English author
and playwright (1867–1933)*

I came across a photograph of him not long ago . . . his black face, the long snout sniffing at something in the air, his tail straight and pointing, his eyes flashing in some momentary excitement. Looking at a faded photograph taken more than forty years before, even as a grown man, I would admit I still missed him.

—*Willie Morris, author and editor (1934–1999)*

The one best place to bury a good dog is in the heart of his master.　　　—*Ben Hur Lampman, writer (1886–1954)*

 Old men miss many dogs.

—*Steve Allen, comedian and entertainer (b. 1921)*

The best way to get over a dog's death is to get another soon.

—*Ronald Reagan, actor and 40th president of the United States (b. 1911)*

Soon or late, every dog's master's memory becomes a graveyard; peopled by wistful little furry ghosts that creep back unbidden, at times, to a semblance of their olden lives. —*Albert Payson Terhune, author (1872–1942)*

For the soul of every living thing is in the hand of God.
—*Job 12:10*

In death they were not parted.
—*2 Samuel 1:23*

Jason Oliver C. Smith, a big dumb guy who was tan, died March 30 of lung cancer and old age. . . . He was 13 years old and lived in New Jersey, Pennsylvania. . . . At the time of his death, his license was current and he had had all of his shots. . . . He is survived by two adults, three children, a cat named Daisy who drove him nuts, and his lifelong companion, Pudgy, whose spaying he always regretted, as well as a host of fleas who have gone elsewhere, probably to Pudgy. . . . He will be missed by all, except Daisy. . . . He never bit anyone, which is more than you can say for most of us.

[Obituary for her golden retriever]
—Anna Quindlen, columnist (b. 1953)

One last word of farewell, dear master and mistress. Whenever you visit my grave, say to yourselves with regret but also happiness in your hearts at the remembrance of my long happy life with you: "Here lies one who loves us and whom we loved." No matter how deep my sleep I shall hear you, and not all the power of death can keep my spirit from wagging a grateful tail.

[From the last will and testament of Blemie O'Neill, the author's beloved dalmatian]
—Eugene O'Neill, playwright (1888–1953)